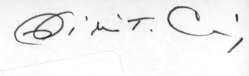

$c

# MIDDLE CLASS FAMILIES

INTERNATIONAL LIBRARY OF SOCIOLOGY

AND SOCIAL RECONSTRUCTION

Founded by Karl Mannheim

Editor W. J. H. Sprott

A catalogue of books available in the INTERNATIONAL LIBRARY OF
SOCIOLOGY AND SOCIAL RECONSTRUCTION and new books in
preparation for the Library will be found at the end of this volume

# MIDDLE CLASS FAMILIES

*Social and Geographical Mobility*

by

COLIN BELL

LONDON

ROUTLEDGE & KEGAN PAUL LTD

NEW YORK: HUMANITIES PRESS

*Published in Great Britain 1968*
*by Routledge and Kegan Paul Ltd*
*Broadway House, 68–74 Carter Lane*
*London, E.C.4*

1969
*Printed in Great Britain by*
*Butler and Tanner Ltd*
*Frome and London*

*SBN 7100 6013 0*

For
JOCELYN, RACHEL
AND LUKE

'It is certainly of service to a man to know who were his grandfathers and who were his grandparents if he entertain an ambition to move in the upper circles of society, and also of service to be able to speak of them as persons who were themselves somebodies in their time. No doubt we all entertain great respect for those who by their own energies have raised themselves in the world; and when we hear that the son of a washerwoman has become Lord Chancellor or Archbishop of Canterbury we do, theoretically and abstractedly, feel a higher reverence for such self-made magnate than for one, who has been as it were born into forensic or ecclesiastical purple. But not the less must the off-spring of the washerwoman have had very much trouble on the subject of his birth, unless he has been, when young as well as when old, a very great man indeed. After the goal has been absolutely reached, and the honour and the titles and the wealth actually won, a man may talk with some humour, even with some affection, of the maternal tub;—but while the struggle is going on, with the conviction strong upon the struggler that he cannot be altogether successful unless he be esteemed a gentleman, not to be ashamed, not to conceal the old family circumstances, not at any rate be silent, is difficult. And the difficulty is certainly not less if fortunate circumstances rather than hard work and intrinsic merit have raised above his natural place an aspirant to high social position. Can it be expected that such a one when dining with a duchess shall speak of his father's small shop, or bring into the light of day his grandfather's cobbler's awl? And yet it is difficult to be altogether silent! It may not be necessary for any of us to be always talking of our parentage. We may be generally reticent as to our uncles and aunts, and may even drop our brothers and sisters in our ordinary conversation. But if a man never mentions his belongings among those with whom he lives, he becomes mysterious, and almost open to suspicion. It begins to be known that nobody knows anything of such a man, and even friends become afraid. It is certainly convenient to be able to allude, if it be but once in a year, to some blood relation.'

ANTHONY TROLLOPE
*The Prime Minister*, pp. 1 and 2
November 1875

wing to production
lays this book was
published in 1969

# Contents

# Contents

# List of Tables

# List of Tables

# List of Diagrams

# Preface

The first debt that any author must acknowledge in a study of this kind is to the families that form the basis of this report. I was met with almost constant courtesy and some curiosity. The estates where they lived have both changed considerably with additional building; also personal details have occasionally been altered to avoid the risk of identification. The genealogies of the three families in Chapter Five are reproduced with their permission and knowledge; their names and all names in the book are fictitious.

My second debt is to the School of Social Studies, University College, Swansea, from which the research was carried out and in which it was written up. I have particular debts to the stimulating comments of Mrs. Margaret Stacey; to Mr. Chris Harris who showed it was possible to make sense of such a mass of data; to Dr. Joe Loudon who made me realize that the obvious was not always the best explanation. Most of all there was the encouragement of my supervisor, Professor W. M. Williams, who provided the original idea. The stylistic infidelities that remain in this book would be even more numerous but for his efforts. My fellow research students: Mrs. Roisin Pill (née Riordan) and Dr. David Robinson, provided much more than a pleasant working atmosphere. My present colleagues in Banbury: Mrs. Anne Murcott and Mr. Eric Batstone have read earlier drafts and made helpful comments. Mrs. Jane Forge (née Hubert) of the London School of Economics was of great assistance in discussing the handling of kinship material.

My greatest debt is to my family: both of origin and marriage. Without their assistance, this book would not have been written.

It goes without saying that responsibility for what follows is mine and mine alone.

*Banbury, December 1967*                                            C. B.

# CHAPTER ONE

# Introduction

The origin of the research on which this book is based is with the most important advance in stratification theory since Lockwood's concept of 'work situation': Watson's concept of 'spiralism'. In his article: 'Social Mobility and Social Class in Industrial Communities' (1964) he introduced the term 'spiralism' for a particular kind of social mobility. The term refers to 'the progressive ascent of . . . specialists of different skills through a series of higher positions in one or more hierarchical structures, and the concomitant residential mobility through a number of communities at or more steps during the ascent,' which results in 'a characteristic combination of social and spatial mobility' (1964, p. 147). Watson contrasts 'spiralists' with what he calls 'burgesses' 'whose limited scale of operations usually restrict them to a specific community . . . (and) are tied to a local community' (p. 149). This research was directly orientated towards those members of the middle class with different mobility experiences, i.e. spiralists and burgesses.

It has recently been commented that the working class are those that the sociologist writes about most but mixes with least (Frankenberg: 1966(a)). The reverse is unfortunately also true and as middle class mobility is often part of the sociologist's own experience it is a perilous subject about which to write. The middle class occupy a peculiar position in British sociology: illustrated for example by their relegation to a footnote but inclusion in a paradigm 'because their presence gives it a certain pleasing symmetry' (Lockwood: 1966, p. 264). In this book I hope to make a start to correct this imbalance in this discussion of social class in Britain.

The research allowed the application of some of the methods of social anthropology in modern urban Britain and made it possible to provide data of a different kind to previous studies of social mobility. The simple re-application of the classical theories and methods with the resources available, in time and money, would not have been satisfactory or satisfying. This led to the emphasis on the centrality of detailed enquiry in an empirical setting. I rely far more than is usual in a study of social mobility on the methods of social anthropology and concentrate to a great extent on what has become known as intra-generational mobility or work life/career mobility.

Because social mobility has not been studied in this way before, it is necessary to outline my methods and the obstacles encountered in the first chapter. Also, I briefly set the local scene and make some more general theoretical comments on the nature of the middle class career pattern. It is around the concepts elaborated there that I organize the empirical data collected for the 120 families studied.

After this introductory chapter there follows the six chapters which form the core of the book. The second and third chapters present the facts of social and geographical mobility. The next four chapters analyse the effects of mobility as outlined in the second and third chapters, firstly on the extended family and secondly on the social relationships on the two estates.

It could be argued that the first part of the book is concerned with what is largely the man's world, that of occupation and career, that this is followed by the family which is shared by both men and women, and that lastly there is what, at least superficially is the women's world, the estates. It is however neither very accurate nor very helpful to look at the problem of social mobility in this way. Career patterns affect the structure[1] and the function of the middle class extended family and the structure of social relationships on the estates.

[1] Throughout this book, when I refer to 'structure' I follow as far as possible Radcliffe-Brown (1952, p. 190) who wrote in his paper 'On Social Function', '. . . direct observation does reveal . . . that . . . human beings are connected by a complex network of social relations'. I use the term 'social structure' to denote this *network of actually existing social relations.* '. . . I regard as a part of the social structure all social relations of person to person.' An example of its usage is given by Firth who wrote in his *Elements of Social Organization* (1951, p. 32), 'In the types of society ordinarily studied

2

Introduction

Perhaps it would be wise to state very briefly my basic orientation towards social class in urban Britain. I think that it contains two major systems, each one of which is related to separate organizational systems, firstly that of the work system and secondly that of the family. I hope that this small piece of research will go some way towards providing a basis for discussion of their interrelationships, and more ambitiously provide the beginnings of a working model for a small segment of urban society.

## 1 Research Design and Methods

Through much modern sociological research there seems to run a dichotomy between the 'quantitative' and the 'qualitative'; between 'hard' data and 'real and deep' data (see Zeldich: 1962). An illustration of this is Stein's fantasy dialogue between Wright Mills and Lazarsfeld. Wright Mills reads to Lazarsfeld the first line of his *The Sociological Imagination*: 'Nowadays men often feel that their private lives are a series of traps.' Lazarsfeld interrupts him and asks 'How many men? which men? how long have they felt this way? which aspects of their private lives bother them? when do they feel free rather than trapped? what kind of traps do they experience? etc., etc.' (Vidich, Bensman and Stein: 1964, p. 215). In this country the dichotomy is often represented by what are loosely thought of as the methods of the sociologists on the one hand and the social anthropologists on the other. But like many dichotomies this one is false, because data should be both 'hard' and 'real and deep'. Social mobility has been largely studied by quantitative methods and the collection of 'hard' data; this research is not in this tradition.

Originally my aim was to construct two sampling frames, one for the geographically mobile members of the middle class, one for the geographically immobile. It might have been possible to define ecological areas in Swansea characterized by a high proportion of each category (initially by the rate index developed

by anthropologists, the social structure may include critical or basic relationships arising similarly from a class system based on relations with the soil. Other aspects of social structure arise through membership in either kinds of persistent groups, such as class, castes, age-sets or secret societies. Other basic relations again are due to position in a kinship system . . .'

B 3

by Herbert (1961)). Then by pilot surveys within specific areas to identify the categories that were required and to sample within them. Not unexpectedly this proved to be an unfertile method, which fortunately pointed the way to the eventual solution.

Firth in his introduction to the L.S.E. Monograph on kinship in London wrote that,

> in applying his intensive techniques of first hand research to the complex conditions of western society the anthropologist has of necessity to break up the field . . . (he) must proceed by differentiating groups, categories, rural and urban, working class, middle class or using the criteria of residential scale, e.g. a block of flats or dispersed housing estates (1956, p. 22).

Frankenberg more recently has argued that

> However large scale the society we wish to study and however massive the residential units, there is always social interaction in small face to face groups . . . (which) . . . gives us the opportunity to observe in microcosm and dynamically the often slow moving and diffuse processes of complex industrial society (1966(a), p. 149).

It indeed proved profitable to take a small contiguous area and treat it as a universe, interviewing intensively within it. New private housing estates were found to be suitable if chosen with care. Watson wrote in the article cited above

> larger communities tend to have socially distinct residential areas and many spiralists live together in suburbs and commute to work. These suburbs may be regarded as specialized residential local communities made up entirely of business and professional people with similar incomes and interests. *Such residential areas have rarely been studied in Britain* (my emphasis). When place of residence and place of work are so closely demarcated and distinct from one another, social relations between varied occupational and economic groups are bound to differ from those that occur in local communities where residence of a wide range of occupational groups is contiguous. The existence of suburban concentrations of occupational groups of all kinds presents analytical problems of social relations and mobility of a different order from those in the local community (1964, p. 151).

As part of the previous ecological exercise all the new private housing estates had been marked on a map of Swansea and the number of houses on each noted. (This was important because there was a limit to the number of households a single unaided research worker could study as intensively as was required. This limit was between 100 and 150.) Pilot studies were carried out on several estates to establish firstly whether in fact they contained both geographically mobile and immobile members of the middle class, whether the kind of intensive research that was envisaged would be possible in such a setting and thirdly whether the results would justify their possible unrepresentativeness.

The pilot survey showed that such research was possible on the estates and that valuable data could be obtained about social mobility and family relations that would be difficult to collect by the more conventional survey methods. From the pilots it seemed that the local middle class would be under-represented in such a study; but happily this turned out to be the result of inefficient and inadequate piloting. Therefore it was decided to begin field work on two new and privately owned housing estates. Two estates were chosen, one with 92 houses, the other with 31, three households refused an interview throughout the fieldwork and so unless otherwise specified all figures throughout this book refer to the 120 households which were interviewed at least once.

A house-to-house census was carried out on both estates, based on the *aide mémoire*, reproduced as Appendix B. This allowed a uniform collection of the basic quantifiable data concerning the demography of the households together with their occupational, residential and educational histories; plus details of kin contact and distribution. This survey, together with the collection of 32 complete genealogies, although valuable, was more useful as a fieldwork technique for the observation of people *in situ* and for establishing a role which was acceptable to them and for allowing intimate observation of certain aspects of their behaviour. The conventional ethnographic methods epitomized by Evans-Pritchard's classic phrase 'to get to know well the persons involved and to see and hear what they say and do', were followed as far as possible. The procedures used on these two estates result from the compromises that had to be made in this particular fieldwork situation: privately owned middle class housing developments in the 1960's in Britain.

5

In this situation the 'anthropological stool' method is not practical. Even if it had been financially possible, living on either of these estates would not have served any great purpose. It would have been difficult to be a member of opposing cliques and the role of the fieldworker would have also been that of neighbour; two that it would in fact have been very difficult to combine. I moved back a stage and relied to a great extent on informants who were themselves participants in events that were of interest. This means that methodologically a great deal depends upon the quality of informants and the fieldworker's skill in evaluating the material they provide. Informants were not used until after the survey and so it was possible to at least have some idea of how they fitted in to sub-systems on the estate.

In the selection of key informants, although every attempt must be made to ensure that they are as representative as possible, an equally important factor is their willingness to play this role. Informants were used representing what were seen as the major categories on the estates: men, women, locals, non-locals, informants at different stages in the family cycle, and where possible at all four stages in the family cycle. Vidich (1954) suggests that the fieldworkers should make use of individuals who are socially marginal to the social system being studied. No deliberate attempt was made to select marginal individuals on the estates, indeed every effort was made to make sure they were as representative as possible of different groups but three of the most willing informants thought of themselves as marginal to the estate and were very astute observers. These three had opted out of life on the estate but could articulate what was happening, e.g. one of the marginal informants pointed out that the role of children as information spreaders and gatherers differed between locals and non-locals (spiralists and burgesses)—the non-locals using their children to a far greater extent. But for sheer quantity of data those informants who were at the hub of interaction were more valuable.

At the risk of appearing trite it must be remembered that in any anthropological field situation the fieldworker has to establish a relationship with his subjects. It is very difficult to observe the pattern of social relations without being part of this pattern, except in some experimental small group situations. It is essential to assume some position in the structure of social relationships. In the more usual anthropological fieldwork situation, the fieldworker is identified as a trader, missionary, colonial officer or foreign spy; any role with which the population has had previous contact and experience. The fieldworker must be placed in a meaningful role by the population he is studying and within a context meaningful to them. Until this happens, whilst there is considerable role confusion, intensive fieldwork is very difficult.

On these two estates, the initial fieldwork was most difficult. This I now recognize, but did not then, as a result of this role confusion. It was necessary in fact to create the role of sociological research worker, and when this role had been established, the fieldwork became a great deal easier.

Associated with the need to create a satisfactory role is the problem of 'sophistication'; by which is meant the process by which individuals who are being studied become self-conscious and give distorted reports of their normal behaviour, and also behave differently because they know they are being studied. This problem was particularly acute because of the role in which the fieldworker had cast himself. As the contact with the estate was not the usual relatively fleeting one of the social surveyors it was necessary to explain in some detail what was being done. This was in an environment where quasi-sociological terms were already in common parlance: 'status seeking' only being the most common. Towards the end of the fieldwork, which lasted seven months on the larger estate, some of the data began to have the air of 'self-fulfilling prophecy' about it. An informant gave an explanation of behaviour in terms of 'inner-direction' and 'other-direction', and another referred to 'joint conjugal roles'. Fieldwork was concluded when an informant said that she had been to a coffee party where the hostess had apologized for inviting her at such short notice but her sociologist was calling tomorrow and she wanted something to tell him.

Frankenberg (1963) described the central paradox of intensive fieldwork and participant observation as seeking information by not asking questions. A participant observer suffers from all the implied evils of self deception, asking questions on the basis of what is already known. As Oscar Lewis has written 'there is a great danger that one will judge the quality of their interpersonal relationships by how they act in relationship to oneself.

This is not necessarily the case' (1951, p. xvii). It is possible to solve this particular problem by very careful and detailed fieldwork over several months. A particular safeguard is to listen very carefully to the questions that are asked, e.g. I found that there was great interest in my position at the University, in how I had got to this position, in what I would do when the research was finished and written up; in other words my career pattern. From this I arrived at the central theme around which it was possible to organize the analysis of the processes of social mobility: that of career, and from this it was a short step to the idea of there being differing *contexts* of social mobility.

A dozen informants kept a diary of who they saw, met and what they did for a month. Methodologically the analysis of these diaries is based on a technique used by Epstein (1961). He gives in great detail his assistant, Chanda's account of who he meets whilst going about his normal business in Ndola in Zambia. He then uses this account to draw attention to various relationships in the urban social structure (extracts from these diaries are quoted in Chapter Six). Following Mayer's valuable terminological discussion these relationships which are ego or family orientated are called *sets*. 'It is made up of people brought into contact in a variety of situations and over a period of time' (1966, p. 102). The combination of these sets on the estate can be built up to give a picture of the *network* of social relationships for the estate. Clyde Mitchell has recently argued that once a standardized method of recording sets and networks can be established they may well play the role in urban societies that genealogies at present play in tribal societies (1966, p. 56). Even more importantly for the purpose of this research Gluckman and Eggan have written that 'the network and other forms of quasi-group which are ego-centred are becoming significant in bridging the gap between structural framework and individual action' (1966, p. xxxv). This is particularly relevant for a study of social mobility, which by common consent is a 'process' but most of the classic studies of social mobility, e.g. Glass (1954) and Lipset and Bendix (1959) do not study a process but the structural framework within which mobility operates (see Frankenberg's (1966) similar point). Whereas structural analysis defines the elements of a social system and the formal relations which bind one status to another, process analysis seeks to des-

8

cribe what actually takes place in the complex web of human interaction. By the study of sets and networks of members of the middle class it is hoped that a new approach can be suggested towards social mobility.

As well as attempting to collect material about quasi-groups 32 genealogies were also collected. More were not collected because of lack of time and a feeling that they were of greater value as a fieldwork technique than for themselves. Those collected were either in connection with ceremonial occasions, e.g. Christenings, or because it seemed that they would be particularly interesting, e.g. because the kin network was very large or very small, or very localized. Three assumptions were made in collecting kin information: firstly, that all the kin given by informants are recognized kin; secondly, the genealogies are complete in as far as they include all the individuals with whom the informant has social relations of any kind; and lastly, that the kindred who are known but not recognized are of negligible importance in the analysis of kinship as a basis for social activity (Williams: 1963, p. 153). A genealogy can be used to place all individuals that the married couple regard as related to them in time and space: both social and geographical.

To conclude, this is a study of social mobility amongst 120 middle class families. It is based on fieldwork on two new private housing estates and it is hoped it will contribute to three sociological areas which correspond to the major sub-divisions of the book. Firstly, that of social mobility, in particular what is usually called intragenerational mobility or work life mobility. Secondly, of the family, in particular the structure and function of the middle class extended family. And thirdly, for want of a better term the ethnology of the two estates. The approach was similar in spirit to that advocated by Arensburg towards community studies. He wrote 'community study is a device for coming to grips with social and psychological facts in the raw. It is a tool of social science, not a subject matter' (1965, p. 30). These two estates were not studied for their own sake but as a way of getting at social mobility 'in the raw'. It is hoped to show that some of the techniques of social anthropology can be applied to modern urban Britain in describing the processes of social mobility.

## 2 *The Local Scene*

Swansea is just one small part of Provincial Britain, part of that outer, darker region, source of funny accents. Its role in social and geographical mobility is that although it may appear in the first chapters of the autobiographies of the famous it rarely appears in the last. Provincial Britain is somewhere to get away from, but recently at least there has been a flow in the other direction. This book is concerned with this mobility especially of members of the middle class.

It is not unusual for studies such as this to begin by regretting the lack of previous work. Happily as far as the local scene is concerned this is not the case. Swansea is no longer sociological *terra incognita*. Indeed in many ways there is an embarrassment of riches, and one must avoid seduction by Dylan Thomas and Kingsley Amis.

A recent survey of the literature edited by Lloyd and Thomason and published under the title of *Welsh Society in Transition* (1963) performed a valuable bibliographical function and so attention will be concentrated mainly on that which has been published since. However it is necessary to mention the pioneer survey by Brennan, Cooney and Pollins: *Social Change in South West Wales*, which still repays careful reading (although it is difficult to agree with MacRae who has called it 'in many ways the most rewarding of post-war British surveys') (1961, p. 75).

More recently there has been the body of research associated with the Lower Swansea Valley Project under the direction of K. J. Hilton; and in particular the reports submitted by Mrs. Margaret Stacey and Mrs. Suzanne Spence on human ecology and housing and the economic structure respectively. Slightly less relevant but valuable in adding a perspective is the geographical synthesis edited by Gerald Manners: *South Wales in the Sixties*. The contemporary political background has been ably summarized in a constituency survey of Swansea West by K. V. Morgan in Butler and King's *The British General Election. 1964.*

Most important however is the recent major work by Colin Rosser and C. C. Harris: *Family and Social Change*, which was based on a 2% sample of the households in the borough. My debt to this work, as a source of both data and ideas is very great. Also methodologically it has eased several problems by allowing intercalibration.[1]

Because these studies, based on far greater resources than I could call upon, have outlined the basic facts of the economic and social systems in South Wales, I will here only attempt to outline a single major theme. It has been described impressionistically by Goronwy Rees in an article with the somewhat loaded title of 'Have the Welsh a Future?':

> . . . a new world and a new society are coming into being as a result of the industrial renaissance of South Wales. Even the democratic class structure of Wales is changing. It is losing its homogeneity and uniformity, based on the preponderance of a single class whether of the peasant or the proletariat and tends increasingly to adapt itself to the subtly graded social hierarchy which provides the anatomy of modern industrial society (1964, p. 12).

One of the agents of this change is the influx of English immigrants.[2] Both the reports of Mrs. Spence and Mrs. Stacey for the Lower Swansea Valley Project document this influx. Mrs. Stacey in her housing report wrote of the estate that she calls 'Private West' that it 'gives the impression that here is an occupationally and socially mobile group, or at any event a group who do not see their future in a house of this kind' (1965, p. 171). This however may have unexpected results for as Mrs. Spence notes 'managers of branch firms are likely to be transferred at the discretion of head office and this may affect their sense of "belonging" to the locality. Whatever the effect of this on the managerial efficiency of the firm there is likely to be a "social" effect, in that branch managers are less likely to become involved in local affairs or to bring their weight to the

[1] Intercalibration has been defined by Southall as relating the distribution of objective criteria thought to be relevant among the subjects of intensive study to their average distribution in the population as a whole and in particular relevant categories as revealed by samples. The degree of representativeness of the persons intensively studied will then be known. The result is that all the qualitative data will refer to a sample of known representativeness in terms of the major quantifiable criteria, although the sample was not randomly drawn (1961, p. 27).

[2] See data presented in Brennan, Cooney and Pollins op. cit., p. 53. W. E. Minchinton, Chapter 1 of Manners op. cit., p. 25. K. O. Morgan op. cit., p. 276. Manners 'Service industry and regional economic growth', *Town Planning Review*, Vol. 33, 1963. Spence op. cit., p. 99.

local scene' (1965, p. 89). She found that 'managers found it difficult to recruit into their own ranks locally' (1965, p.100). Manners more generally has argued that 'the immediate future of the Swansea sub-region will probably see the continued net loss of population through emigration although it is equally likely that the counterflow of professional, managerial and technically skilled people, drawn west by the new industries and service jobs in and around Swansea, will persist' (1965, p. 65). In a series of articles on the 'State of the Nation' *The Guardian* quoted 'an observer who knows local industry intimately' who 'noted that on the whole middle as well as top management tends to be English rather than native Welsh' (Article by Nesta Roberts: 18.2.1965).

Locally they live side by side with the local middle class. Ecological segregation by class is as characteristic of Swansea as of any other town of its size in Britain (see section on Swansea in Harold Carter's: *The Towns of Wales*, 1965). Raymond Williams has said (in a conversation with Richard Hoggart):

> the stratification at work is reproduced physically in the new communities. You can see it at Margam: this really beautiful making of steel and everything round it ugly as hell. The main workers' estates are there in the mill's shadow, while the managers and the executives drive away to live in 'unspoiled' places like Gower and Porthcawl (*New Left Review*, No. 1, 1960,).[1]

But their neighbours are often part of what Brennan, Cooney and Pollins called 'the local system'.

Both these sections of the middle class are to be found on the new private housing estates that are rapidly filling in the urban fabric of Swansea especially on the western side. Two such estates were chosen for study but before the different mobility experiences of the families living on them are analysed it is necessary to consider the middle class career pattern from a more theoretical standpoint.

---

[1] For academic confirmation of this see Spence op. cit., p. 50: 'it seems likely that the persons living in Swansea West and travelling out of the borough are in part the staff and managerial workers of the Steel Company of Wales and other manufacturing industries located outside the Borough, who live in this residential part of Swansea'.

## 3 Middle Class Career Patterns

In Max Weber's classic discussion of the nature of bureaucracy he noted that 'career advance . . . is organized in "a system of promotions" according to seniority or to achievement or both' (1947, p. 334). It is this concept of 'career advance' that I want to discuss here because it is not only limited to bureaucrats but permeates the whole middle class life style; and has particular relevance to any discussion of middle class social mobility.

A career creates its own inexorable logic: it holds out the prospects of continuing predictable rewards, develops a willingness to train and to adopt a long time perspective and to defer immediate gratification (Scheider and Lysgaard 1955, Strauss 1962, and B. G. Stacey, 1965). In Mannheim's phrase it leads to the gradual creation of a 'life-plan' (1940, pp. 56, 104–6 and 181).

The nature of the middle class career may perhaps be emphasized by a brief comparison with that of the working class. It is an aspect of what Lockwood has called the 'work situation' (1958, p. 15). Ely Chinoy's analysis of the life cycles of American car workers shows that 'Two ladders of advancement seem to have emerged in industry. One, open to workers, is short with few rungs, usually ending in foremanship. The other open to those whose education and training enable them to train as technicians or white-collar workers, is longer and may eventually lead to top levels of industry' (1955, p. 6). And 'Unlike the professional or the salaried office holder, the factory worker does not see his present job as part of a career pattern which channels his aspirations and sustains his hope' (1955, p. 117). Richard Hoggart's penetrating discussion of the working class milieu, notes that there is 'lack of scope for the growth of ambition . . . once at work there is for most no sense of career . . . life is not seen as a climb' (1955, p. 62). (Compare this with the situation in Crestwood Heights, Toronto: 'to the people of Crestwood Heights the career is of all concerns the most momentous' (Seeley, Sim and Loosley, 1963, p. 118). As Dahrendorf argues, in what he calls 'post-capitalist' society, 'a fairly clear as well as significant line can be drawn between salaried employees who occupy positions that are part of a bureaucratic hierarchy and those in positions that are not' (1959,

p. 55).[1] So middle class people have a far greater potential for intragenerational mobility than do members of the working class.

Watson in his important paper makes the point that most middle class people 'enter into life-careers of an almost identical pattern, whatever the nature of their work and the considerable variation in salaries. This pattern is a progress up the ladder of promotion through competition for higher posts with greater responsibility and with higher salaries and prestige'(1964, pp. 144–5). This pattern of advance may or may not entail geographical mobility, but if it does, it is accepted because of the centrality of the career in the middle class life style. The career provides the reference group and gives continuity to personal life experience. As Weiss and Reisman have argued

> One's career is not merely the trace-line of one's journey through life—a running record of places and statuses, tasks and rewards; a skeleton autobiography. It may also furnish a rationale for life, a sense of whether one's work is related to one's ultimate aims and one's growing abilities. The professional and managerial occupations are unique in that they permit the individual to hope that his effort will be cumulative, that his jobs taken all together may represent a coherent contribution to some end (1963).

And they point out that in both professional and managerial fields there is strong pressure to evaluate success in terms of a career, a sequence of jobs which in the ideal should be ever increasing in responsibility and prestige.[2] As a result of advancement with age, there is always a means of comparison, it is always possible to see if one is 'falling behind one's salary'. The

---

[1] A similar point is made by R. Hamilton, *B.J.S.*, 1963, 'The Income difference between Skilled and White Collar Workers' who points out that even if income differences between white-collar and skilled workers are lessened there remain differences in career pattern.

[2] Also see J. A. Kahn: *The American Class Structure* (1957), pp. 193–201, for a textbook synthesis of the importance of career in 'upper-middle' class lives.

Erving Goffman: in *Asylums* (1963), p. 127, has interestingly suggested that although 'the term career has been reserved for those who expect to enjoy the rises laid out within a respectable profession' it is coming to be used however 'in a broadened sense to refer to any social strand of any person's course through life'. In this section I am talking about career in the traditional sense but later on I realize that I am in fact going some way to describe a 'social strand'.

'high-class' Sunday newspapers encourage mobility. In the words of one informant, 'You'd be surprised at the number of people you'd find in the office on a Monday morning, thumbing through the Sunday papers, just making sure the grass on the other side of the fence is not just that bit greener.'

The career is the context within which the mobility of these 120 middle class families are studied. For them it is 'the supreme social reality' (Dahrendorf: 1959, p. 56). But as Lipset has noted 'for the middle classes . . . age is largely correlated with career . . . the older a person (up to a certain age) the more likely he is to have moved up in social-economic position' (1963, p. 264).[1] For the sociologist working on the outside, as it were, as opposed to the industrial sociologist working on the inside, this makes it very difficult to distinguish between the rewards of seniority and the rewards of ability. This is not a study of the structure of opportunity, of the actual organization of the company, although I recognize this may affect career patterns. For example it has been said that

> Unilever is a collection of small pyramids constantly changing their size and position and forming zig-zag routes to the peak. A man in Unilever can (and has) become managing director of Walls Sausages at the age of 28 and from there might move through soap, timber and toothpaste up to the Central Board (Sampson, 1965, p. 460).

The career is taken as given, and its effects on the structure of social relationships are analysed.

The effects of differing career patterns, and of differing potential for mobility has recently been graphically shown by Sykes. In the firm he studied all 96 clerks thought 'prospects' were more important than 'pay', compared with 12 out of 118 manual workers. He demonstrates that clerks and manual workers have very different attitudes to social mobility (and here he is talking about intragenerational mobility) 'Clerks thought that promotion would cause no social problems at work or at home whereas the majority of manual workers

---

[1] See also H. F. Lydall and D. G. Tipping: 'The Distribution of Personal Wealth in Britain', *Oxford U. Inst. of Stats. Bul.*, 23 (1961), p. 95, and Table IX, p. 96, and J. A. Banks: *Moving up in Society*, Twentieth Century, May 1960, pp. 25–6.

thought it would cause social problems at both'. He concluded that 'clerks and manual workers have a different industrial ethos' (compare Lockwood's 'work situation') which he sees as having grown out of the fact of having or not having opportunities for promotion. In summation he says

> It would appear . . . that the lack of opportunities for promotion had caused the manual workers to develop very rigid class boundaries and a rejection of upward social mobility for themselves and for other manual workers. The clerks on the other hand had no such rigid class boundaries and set a value on upward social mobility for themselves and for other clerks.

But he points out that

> the rejection of social mobility by the manual workers appeared to apply only to the industrial situation. In Scotland social class is flexible and several of the manual workers interviewed had relatives who were doctors, lawyers, teachers, ministers or held other professional or clerical posts. This was regarded as a subject for pride not for concealment. Thus it would appear that the rejection of social mobility relates only to promotion within industry, not to upward social mobility by other means (1965, p. 302).

It should be noted here that he is apparently confusing intra-generational mobility with inter-generational mobility. It is very unlikely that any of the doctors or lawyers began their working lives as manual workers. But I would want to argue that just as Sykes shows that there is a strong *rejection* of intragenerational mobility by manual workers, there is a strong *expectation* of intra generational mobility by middle class workers (see Runciman, 1966).

It has been shown that in studies of intra-generational mobility there appear to be two contradictory underlying assumptions. In their paper Tausky and Dubin (1965) argue that these are firstly, that men are oriented towards career long advance: this they call the unlimited success theory and they quote Parsons, Lipset and Bendix, Veblen and Reisman. Secondly, that men are oriented towards stabilizing or modestly improving their occupational rank; this they call the limited success theory and they quote Everett Hughes, Whyte and C. Wright Mills. They surmount this problem by developing what they call a 'career anchorage model' of mobility which involves either the recognition that one's occupational life history is part of a career (upward career anchorage) or a point of reference from which present or future occupational position may be evaluated (downward career anchorage). Their general model of motivation requires that a career perspective be anchored at some reference point which may be either the starting point of a career or the level of maximum possible achievement. This career anchorage model is valuable because it allows for the divergent reference points that I found amongst the families I studied. Most of these families in fact had an upward career anchorage model if only because they are mainly still young: the older the man (and consequently usually the greater the work-life mobility experienced) the more likely that they had a downward orientation.

A second concept related to career that was of value to my analysis, is Litwak's 'ordered change' (1960($d$)).[1] The career by definition is composed of a more or less orderly and predictable set of stages in which each is a prerequisite to what follows. If change is ordered around a career it is possible for the individual to view both his current membership group and his future membership group as reference groups without endangering his integration into his current group and without preventing his joining a future group. Litwak would argue that 'High membership turnover in primary groups will be consistent with primary group cohesion where the individual has a *stepping stone reference orientation* and where the change is an ordered one'.

Litwak utilizes these concepts to explain how some neighbourhoods, despite high membership turnover, develop high cohesion—for example that described in *The Organization Man* (Whyte, 1963). On the two estates that I studied there were two groups of families: those who expected to be geographically mobile in the course of their career and those who did not. The neighbouring patterns of these two groups was different, in part this could be explained by the concept of 'ordered change'.

In Crestwood Heights the effects of this stepping-stone

[1] See also his 'Reference Group Theory, Bureaucratic Career and neighbourhood Primary Group Cohesion', *Sociometry*, Vol. 23 (1960), pp. 72–84.

reference orientation are elaborated (Seeley, Loosley and Sim, 1956, p. 155).

> Each person in Crestwood Heights no matter how mobile, finds a place in the social structure where he can work and live: even if he is oriented to go higher, he will, if fortunate, derive satisfaction from the level he occupies at the moment. That level represents a goal achieved. All his possessions, all his associations —formal and informal—help to make his position secure and tenable. He occupies a niche in the division of labor and in the social organization of his society; that niche when compared with all others affords a measure of the success of his career in the stratified competitive world in which he lives.

Moving to the next niche in the division of labour and the social organization of his society often involves geographical mobility: from community to community. It is for this type of social mobility Watson has coined the valuable term 'spiralism'[1]; 'the progressive ascent through a series of higher positions in one or more hierarchical structures with a concomitant residential mobility through a number of communities' (1964, p. 147). Spiralists are seen as a socially, economically and geographically mobile national category, an important by-product of the process of bureaucratization. This combination of mobility in residence, career and social standing is characteristic of managers in the largest concerns. As George Homans explains in a review of *The Organization Man*:

> he expects to move from post to post as the corporation changes his assignments. Accordingly he will not get himself mixed up for long in the affairs of a particular community. He will not hope to become a prominent citizen of Indianapolis but of Standard Oil Co. of Indiana (1962).

Here it is necessary to emphasize a division that runs throughout this study and has already been suggested. A division between what Watson calls spiralists and between what he calls burgesses: whose limited scale of operations usually restrict them to a specific local community. 'Spiralists are distinguished from other professions with the same education

---

[1] Watson (1964), p. 147, and *Twentieth Century*, May 1960, pp. 414–415; see also Susser and Watson: *Sociology in Medicine*, 1962, especially Chapter 4 on Social Mobility, pp. 111–150.

and in the same social class, e.g. solicitors who have practices and take fees and thereby have an economic and professional interest in the area in which they live' (1964, p. 149). All that has been said above concerning the nature of the middle class career pattern applies to both spiralists and burgesses. Geographical mobility is expected by spiralists but not by burgesses.

This division in middle class career patterns is implicit in Crestwood Heights when Seeley, Loosley and Sim qualify the contention that 'for the sake of social mobility and personal advancement an individual must be prepared to leave his family, his neighbourhood, his friends and his colleagues behind as he moves on and up' (p. 139), by pointing out that 'horizontal movement' can be deleterious to a career. Their case study of 'Robert' (p. 458) is a good example of what above is called a 'burgess'. It emphasizes the difference in mobility potential between different segments of the middle class. Although they say that 'a prime requisite of the career is a seemingly effortless mobility . . . personal movement in physical and social space' (p. 119), this is not so for all members of the middle class. There are also the locals or burgesses.[1]

These two groups are difficult to compare in terms of social mobility. The division between spiralists and burgesses adds to the difficulties inherent in such a study. Difficulties put succinctly by Marsh when he said

> In contemporary (American) society there is no one occupation or career which *far more* than all others assures one of the greatest rewards the society has to offer. Prestige, influence, wealth and other rewards are somewhat *dispersed* among several professions, government service, business leadership and politics (1961, p. 1).

How much simpler is the situation he describes in the *Ch'ing* period in China where 'the highest worldly rewards of the

---

[1] See also R. K. Merton's well known discussion of influentials: *Social Theory and Social Structure*, rev. ed., 1957, pp. 387–420. An integral part of his analysis of what he calls 'cosmopolitans' and 'locals' is 'the varying types of career pattern . . . whether they were developed largely within Rovere or were furthered in Rovere after having been initiated elsewhere' (p. 392). But in Merton's terms, not all burgesses are necessarily locals—those I studied certainly were not, and not all spiralists are necessarily cosmopolitans but most of those I studied were. There is however a broad tendency to be able to equate these two sets of terms.

society were all integrated into one ideal career pattern—office in the imperial governmental bureaucracy'. We have the difficulty of comparing different career patterns, which take place in different contexts: of which the community is only one, another is that of one's professional associates, another is that of the organization which employs the individual be it university, business or government. And the career may take place in more than one context. But it must always be seen in a network of social interaction and by a close examination of the social networks of the 120 families living on two private housing estates I hoped it would be possible to analyse their differing contexts of social mobility.

# CHAPTER TWO

# Geographical Mobility

## 1 *Previous Approaches*

Max Weber wrote that 'the "social class" structure is composed of the plurality of class statuses between which an interchange of individuals on a personal basis or in the course of generations is *readily possible and typically observable*' (1947, p. 424) (my emphasis). The study of this readily possible and typically observable interchange of individuals on a personal basis (which I interpret as meaning what is now understood as *intra*-generational mobility) or in course of generations (*inter*-generational mobility), i.e. of social mobility has recently been called 'an outstanding example of cumulative research in modern sociology' (Jackson and Crockett: 1964, p. 5). If not since Weber then since Sorokin in 1927 social mobility has certainly received a great deal of attention. Sorokin's *Social Mobility* was acknowledged in 1954 by D. V. Glass as 'the only comprehensive work' and is still the compulsory starting point for any further work, even if on specific topics it had been superseded. It is however unfortunate that studies of social mobility since Sorokin have not been startling in their originality, in theory, insight or method. They have instead been characterized more by their ingenuity, thoroughness and overwhelming energy, and increasingly sophisticated statistical techniques (see for example the recent edition of *Acta Sociologica* edited by Carlsson and Glass: Vol. 9, parts 1 and 2, 1966).

More specific criticisms of recent studies of social mobility, for which the work of D. V. Glass *et al.* has served as a model will be made in Chapter Three. In this chapter attention will be concentrated upon the previous literature on the geographical mobility of the middle class which is the first concern of this book, on what Sorokin called the 'horizontal intra-occupational circulation of individuals' (1959, p. 394). Sorokin himself was only concerned with manual and skilled manual workers and not at all with the middle class. To our modern (and British) eyes he somewhat surprisingly wrote, 'it is to be expected that the horizontal intra-occupational circulation of other more qualified occupations is somewhat less than of laborers' (p. 397). All the evidence, some of which is presented below, is against Sorokin on this point. (He himself is of course a very fine example of the geographical mobility of the well qualified.)

Macro data on internal migration, or geographical mobility in Britain can be obtained from the 'Migration National Summary Tables' of the census. The following basic facts can be gleaned from the 1961 tables. In 1961 11% of the population of England and Wales had lived in their present residence for less than a year, 34% for less than 5 years and 61% for less than 15 years. In Swansea however there was less residential mobility: 9·4% of the population had lived in their present residence for less than a year, 28% for less than 5 years and 54% for less than 15 years. From the second part of these tables it is possible to distinguish between immigrants and emigrants and those who moved only within the local authority area. The figures for England and Wales in 'per-thousands' (‰) are 51‰ within local authority areas, 47‰ between local authority areas and 7‰ immigrants in 1961. For Swansea the figures are 65‰ within the local authority area and 23‰ emigrants out of it, and 27‰ immigrants into it (giving a positive migration balance of 4‰ or 610 people). As Cullingworth points out 'inter-regional migration . . . is only a minor part of the total complex of movements' (1965, p. 59).[1]

The Census data however are of only limited value to this study as they give no real indication of who actually is moving, why and how far. For these aspects of mobility it is necessary to turn to other sources.

For example Donnison in an article on the movement of

---

[1] For comparative material for the U.S.A. see Rossi (1955) who suggests that one American in five changes his residence every year.

households in England showed that when compared with non-movers, movers included a significantly larger proportion of households with heads in administrative, professional, managerial and skilled manual occupations (1961, p. 62). And 'a comparison according to occupation showed that a change of job was mentioned as a reason for past moves by 42% of households whose heads were in administrative, professional, managerial jobs and by only 11% of those with heads in other occupations' (p. 68). Of particular relevance to this study he wrote that 'the stress laid by the middle class occupational groups upon new jobs as a reason for moving is reflected in the greater distance moved' (p. 69).

Similarly in his study of *Neighbours* Bracey found that nearly 50% of the English private estate dwellers expected to move: in an overwhelming number of cases the reason given was job transfer. 36% had been previously living in distant towns and villages. In every case a transfer of job had been involved and for all but two this had meant a removal of more than 80 miles.

Examples of middle class geographical mobility are easily found. Pahl (1964, p. 47): 'of the Registrar-General's Occupational Group I only 2% were born in the county of Hertfordshire', Loudon (1966, p. 77): 'no adult members of (the middle class) households were born and brought up in the parish' (in the Vale of Glamorgan); Bealey, Blondel and McCann (1965, p. 259) writing about Newcastle-under-Lyme, or Birch (1959, p. 35) writing of Glossop: 'people who get ahead . . . tend to become geographically as well as socially mobile and to join the increasingly large class of professional and managerial workers who have not got any strong roots in any local community'. The example given by Mrs. Stacey in *Tradition and Change*, 'Mr. Brown' is a particularly fine example of a geographically mobile member of the middle class, i.e. a spiralist (1960, p. 17).[1]

Geographical and social mobility are not just a coming together of words. One leads to the other,[2] ('Caste' in the

---

[1] For more journalistic accounts of international geographical mobility see Macrae (1965) and Richmond (1965).

[2] Stouffer (1940) made one of the only serious theoretical efforts to explain geographical mobility when he wrote 'the number of people going a given distance is directly proportional to the number of opportunities at that

23

Southern States of the U.S. was built on a denial of mobility both social and geographical, see for example Dollard (1937)). The migratory aspects of social mobility are often limited to just the facts of physical movement, but it must be remembered that in reality families and individuals usually are moving from one social group to another. The specific problems of the relationships between the 'established' groups and the newcomers, the 'outsiders', has recently been stimulatingly treated by Elias and Scotson. They treat mobility as only having really occurred when an individual and his family moves his home and occupation from one locality to another and has become wholly dependent on the new locality for livelihood and principal social contacts.[1] Hollingshead and Redich recognize that such a group of mobile individuals exist in significant numbers (at least in the U.S.) when they give as one of the defining characteristics of their Class II: 'having moved from their home community to another community, only to be shifted to still other communities by their ambitions. Each advance in geographical and/or social space has taken these families from accustomed milieus and forced them to put down new roots' (1958, pp. 85–6).

The third section in the introductory chapter was concerned with the nature of the middle class career. It is now possible to illustrate further some themes raised in that chapter by giving examples of geographical mobility experienced as part of the middle class career pattern.

There have been very few studies of the relationship between career pattern and geographical mobility. Warner and Abegglen wrote of occupational mobility that 'such mobility may include changes from one job to another within a community, from one job to another between communities and from one type of job to another within or between communities. *On the whole these latter types of movement have not been studied*'

[1] See also Mann (1965), pp. 21–2, who notes the Home Office instruction that Chief Constables should be appointed from outside the local force, thereby encouraging geographical mobility.

distance and inversely proportional to the number of intervening opportunities'. I know of no attempt to apply this and so while it might be possible so to do given accurate and macro statistics, after considerable thought I feel that it is not very helpful.

(1955, p. 13) (my emphasis). They later write though: 'more important to the patterns of occupational mobility than the territorial origins of business leaders is their territorial circulation. Most of these men have been spatially mobile during their careers' (p. 26). Warner and Abegglen underline their position when they write

> It has been assumed that geographical mobility is a necessary step in occupational and social mobility, that movement through social space and the implied break with the family and the class of orientation require sheer physical distance. Certainly the extent of mobility of the business elite would support this assumption (p. 83).

In Watson's original article on spiralism he presented a secondary analysis of Birch's study of Glossop. Here I would like, very briefly, to comment on Warner's study of Morris, Illinois, published under the title of *Democracy in Jonesville* (1949). For in it are contained many of the assumptions about social mobility that are very common, and yet on the evidence that is presented may be questioned. Warner analyses social mobility in Jonesville in a chapter sub-titled 'The Rise and Fall of Families'. Geographical mobility from locality to locality is not dealt with specifically (this would of course be difficult as it is quite likely that those who had been geographically mobile would not 'fit' into a single unified status hierarchy). Later he wrote (of the mill)

> Most of the positions at the top require special skills and must be filled by men who are trained for these jobs. For example the chief scientist came from the East, the engineer came from Detroit, one of the accountants from Alabama and all the people in a managerial position, with the exception of one, were brought in from the outside (p. 113).

So in fact the importance of geographical mobility for the middle class career is noted but it is not elaborated how it affects the local class system, or how they 'fit' into the local social system that is described. In his treatment of social mobility, nepotism is emphasized but geographical mobility which I would expect to be far more important is largely ignored.

A more realistic analysis of mobility has been given by

Goldschmidt, which can be taken as a specific criticism of Warner: 'By focusing attention on the community as a matrix for social action, the dynamic aspects of status are lost. Few families . . . moved upwards within the local community but there are many persons moving in and out . . . on their way up' (1950, p. 1215). Similarly Lipset (1954) has pointed out the atypicality of U.S. community studies as a basis for any generalizations about mobility, either social or geographical.

In this country with notable exceptions, there are very few studies of the relationship between spatial and social mobility. Most data were only collected incidentally. For example in his article 'Religious Order and Mental Disorder: a study of a South Wales Rural Community', Loudon wrote, 'most of the middle class in the parish are people without long standing local attachments who have deliberately moved into the area as part of the process of upward social mobility or as a means of maintaining their own perceived social position in the relative isolation of a small rural community' (1966, p. 95).

Pahl (1964) examined the relationship between geographical and social mobility and found that he could 'question the existence of a "new middle class" who had risen from humble origins through their own merit' (p. 53). Of the 103 middle class chief earners in the households he studied in Hertfordshire 71 came from middle class parents and therefore only 32 came from the working class. More than half of this socially mobile minority came from families where the chief wage earner was a foreman or skilled manual worker. He wrote forcefully that 'the semi-skilled and unskilled manual workers contributed few recruits to the middle class' (p. 54). He does not develop his social mobility material but concludes sensibly that 'the important point is to note that there is no easy correlation between social mobility and geographical mobility. That there may be such a correlation for a minority may be true, however it is certainly a minority which has been socially mobile' (p. 54). I have quoted Pahl at length because as will be shown in Chapter Three, there is a striking similarity between my findings concerning the relationship of social and geographical mobility and his, even though the two studies were carried out in two very different parts of the country.

Another study of the inter-relations of social and geographical mobility is by Musgrove (1963) called *The Migratory Elite*. Not unnaturally for an educational sociologist he stresses the importance of the grammar school for both social and geographical mobility. It is a major contention of his that non-locals will be over-represented in the sphere of local leadership and in the local bureaucracy. He does not explain, however, why some of 'the elite' are not geographically mobile, indeed he largely ignores those who Watson has called 'burgesses' and makes no attempt to analyse the inter-relations between locals and non-locals, after all they are frequently neighbours.

Finally in this very brief description of the previous approaches I must refer to the literature synthesizing work of Lipset and Bendix as a final authority against Sorokin's view of middle class geographical mobility. They write (though in a footnote) 'that professionals and semi-professionals had the highest rate of geographical mobility of any occupational group' (1959, p. 206).

I will turn now to an analysis of the empirical data that was collected on the social and geographical mobility of the 120 middle class households studied.

## 2   Two Career Autobiographies

Altogether six male informants were asked to write short 'career autobiographies' about how and why they became what they are now and how they thought they were going to go on. Two of the six were locals, in that they had been born and bred in Swansea. The other four were non-locals, i.e. they had been geographically mobile; of these four two had also been socially mobile in that their fathers' jobs are normally thought of as working class. All six originally accepted the task, but one of the locals eventually said that he had not got the time, and one of the non-locals decided that although he had written a 'career autobiography' he would not give it to me. Of the remaining four, two are presented here. (My additions, in italics.) The first is by Mr. L., a socially immobile local (i.e. he comes from a middle class background and has always lived in Swansea), and the second by Mr. T., who had been both socially and geographically mobile (i.e. he comes from a working class background in another part of the country). The two career autobiographies must not be considered as 'ideal types' but as what Gluckman has called 'apt-illustrations' (1961, p. 7) for a basis for discussion.

1. Mr. L. 39-year-old wholesaler from a middle class background who had always lived in Swansea.

I think that most people are ambitious, they want a good job and a good home. I was lucky because I started with both. My people have always been comfortably off and as I was the eldest it was always assumed that I, at least, would go into Dad's business. I can remember when I was at school (*the local grammar school*) other boys saying they were going to sea or become professional footballers. I was always going to be a farmer, like my uncles (*father's brothers*)—we used to stay with them during the school holidays. But as it got nearer the time to leave school it became obvious that I would follow my father—as they say.

I am the third generation—we were already 'and son' with my father. I have only got daughters! It was tremendous when I started because I was the boss's son and I thought I could do what I liked. Also as I started at 16 and knew I would have to go into the forces at 18 I did not take those two years very seriously at all.

I was two years in the Air Force: in Scotland and Germany, that was the only time I had lived away from Swansea. When I came back I was not so wild and instead of spending all day messing around in the warehouse and on the lorries I had to learn the business. (I got married three years later when I was 23.)

I will explain the set up. The firm can be divided into two halves: warehouse and office. There are subdivisions in each.

Those who work in the warehouses: about 18 men and those who work on the lorries: about 22 men are all what I suppose you would call working class. But we pay them, especially the three foremen, more than we pay many of those who work in the office. In the office we have 12 clerks who vary in age from two who have just left school, to my chief clerk who is old enough to be my father. There are six girls who work in the office—typing and working the machines. Working outside we have four representatives and six buyers. The representatives going to the shops we supply to sell. I count these ten men as being part of the office staff.

As you are interested in social movement, two of the representatives started in the warehouse. Above them all, in what are known as 'the top offices' are the company secretary, who is an accountant, my younger brother and myself. We three all have our own secretaries.

I will tell you about the division of authority between us three. The company secretary is there to balance the books—really to see that the gap between the price we sell and that at which we buy is large enough to cover costs and make a decent profit. My brother will take his place when he retires and is taking accountancy examinations. He has special responsibility for the office. My special responsibility, although I am overall boss—I hire and fire, is the warehouse. I make sure I go there every day to see the men and make sure things are running smoothly.

But more than that I am the firm's public image. I go round to see the shop-keepers we supply—not to do the representatives' job but to let them see we are interested. I know them all and they knew my dad. I also go to see our suppliers, both locally and more occasionally in London. The local suppliers we have often dealt with since the firm began in 1882. We all know each other. But I think that there is more to it than that—I am the trade's image for people outside the trade. We are after all the biggest firm in the trade in Swansea. So I am a member of Rotary and a very keen one. And I belong to many clubs and associations because I think it is a good thing that other Swansea people see me at the right functions and that we are not just tradesmen. I also belong to several social clubs as a duty really so that I meet the important Swansea people. All this kind of thing is very important in a town like Swansea.

Although I have no paper qualifications I run the firm. This would be very difficult without the goodwill my grandfather and father built up. I try to continue it. Without it we would be less successful. Really I think I mean, without the people we know locally.

About the future—It is very difficult to make predictions because as I have told you the trade is going through a very difficult time. We are under tremendous pressure from outside. In the last year alone I have had an offer for the firm from all three of the major combines outside South Wales. Outside of South Wales the whole trade is divided up by three large combines and their associates but for some reason here it is still in the hands of about 20 firms like mine. I suppose we all ought to get together but until very recently there has never seemed to be a real need. I do not think that we will sell because it was my grandfather's and my father's firm. If we did I would undoubtedly remain as general manager but it would no longer be the same. I would no longer be at the top.

Anyway finally I will say that my future is with the firm and the firm's future is with Swansea. It is both my home and my living. And I could not ask for a better place.


2. Mr. T. 38-year-old chemist from a working class background. He has lived in four towns before Swansea.

There were times when I used to think that I was a cliché—the working class boy who made good, a member of the new middle class, the meritocratic technocrat. The whole question of identity was very difficult for me and my kind. For me all this is no longer a problem because I now think I know where I am going.

In many ways though I must be absolutely typical. My dad was, and is, a railway worker in the railway town in which I was brought up. I went to the grammar school and pushed by dad and the school went on to university—very red brick and provincial (after I had been in the army two years which I hated). Once at University I worked like hell and got a first. I stayed on to do a Ph.D. in chemistry—looking back I think as much as anything to avoid going out into the world. Whilst I was a research student I married and had a child so things were extremely tough financially. It was during this time that I was seduced by 'A' (*large company*) who regularly go round university departments and get at research students. The money they offered me was fantastic, more than my father earns now in five years and I was going to do pure research—or so they said.

We moved to (*the home counties*) to work for them and I stayed for exactly eight months after which I left in high dudgeon about wasting my time. We did not move immediately. I taught for a term in the local 'tech' while I thought things out.

Next I tried scientific journalism for three years in London. We moved into the metropolis when I got the job. In many ways it was very satisfying because it allowed me to keep up with my subject without actually teaching it and without too great a feeling of prostituting myself. But after three years we had two more children and where we were living was no place to bring them up. Also I did not really have a career. I did not know where I was going to be in 20 years.

I applied for what now seems like thousands of jobs and eventually joined the company that I am now with. I suppose I joined them as much as anything because they offered me a job in a part of the country in which I wanted to live: Kent. Also

I could work in organic chemistry an aspect of which I had earlier done research and had published. So we moved and really liked it, both the place and the job. I worked in a sumptuous lab. with plenty of assistants. I could see where I was going. After three years they offered me a job in Holland (in fact I really went after it. It got around that it was in the offing that the company wanted someone to develop a research department). We were in Holland for three years and it was great. The kids learned Dutch and I made my mark.

About then I had to make up my mind about whether I stayed on the research side or moved over. By then I think I was committed to the company. There were greater opportunities on the administrative side of getting a really senior position, but it was and is far more cut-throat. If I stayed on the research side, now was the time to get out and go into a university department for about five years before moving back into industry. As you know I took the risk and moved over onto the administrative side. I thought it would be to my advantage because I had a Ph.D. and it is a company joke that the people who run what after all is a very technologically advanced organization cannot tell their secretaries' typewriters from a catylistic cracker. I also thought that my extra-industrial experience in scientific journalism would stand me in good stead because it at least proved that I was a literate scientist.

I did not get the first job that I went after because I was too junior in the company. Seniority counts a little on the administrative side (not so much on the research and technical side), therefore there is a lot to be gained by getting in early. But I was offered my present position soon afterwards.

We were more than a little dubious at first because it was in Wales, which after Holland we expected to be very drab and 'How Green is my Valley'. We have of course been pleasantly surprised. We could not really have afforded to turn it down because it was a real break for me. I suppose that I am head of a third of a very large plant. Locally I have two peers and one man above me. I do not think that I will really push myself for another couple of years, we will have been here four years by then and will have built up a bit of seniority.

There are five places I could move to from here, four in this country and one in Holland; three of those in this country are basically similar plants to the one at which I now work and I would only go to them as top man. The situation is similar with our Dutch plant. The fourth place in this country is the head office in London. I cannot make up my mind whether it is better to go to London and become really known and then become a local top man, then move back to London, or try to become a local top man first, moving to London later. But now I am as determined as anyone to get on and in the end this will mean going to London. Anyway we will not be here on this estate in five years' time, probably not in South Wales either.

You will have noticed that I now do not think at all of moving to another company. At the moment a move like that could well be disadvantageous, but I do know where I could move to. In fact I know my opposite numbers in other companies but I think I get a better deal with this company and so I think I will stay with them. Unless of course I am still *here* in five years and if I am you can be sure that by then I shall be looking for somewhere else to move to. I do not think that this will happen though.

I have found now that the majority of my friends also work for the same company, certainly all the people I know well in Swansea are really colleagues—and my wife is only really friendly with the wives of my colleagues. This I suppose is yet another reason for not leaving the company.

I know that I have come a long way. I notice it especially when I go home. But mine is a very good company and they can have all the ability I have got. I want to get on but I hope that moving will not interfere with the children's education. But if I can get another couple of notches up I will be able to send the boys to boarding school, not that I really approve of them but it will make moving much easier.

The themes that these two career autobiographies raise centre around the differing contexts of social mobility that are open to members of the middle class. Mr. L. wrote, '. . . my future is with the firm and the firm's future is with Swansea', so making explicit the orientation of the local, what Watson called the 'burgess'. Mr. T. on the other hand wrote, '. . . mine is a very good company and they can have all the ability I have got.' As his own career amply demonstrates his is an international company, not tied to any single locality; he is what Watson called a 'spiralist'.

The effect of the differing context of mobility for these two men on their kin contact is also brought out. Mr. T. has no local kin living in Swansea, whereas Mr. L. has many, and he followed both his father and his grandfather into his firm. He works closely with his brother, whereas Mr. T. has no kinsman working in the rest of the very large organization for which he himself works. On the pattern of friendship, Mr. T. wrote, 'I have found now that the majority of my friends also work for the same company, certainly all the people I know in Swansea are really colleagues—and my wife is only really friendly with the wives of colleagues.' He writes rather ruefully, 'This I suppose is yet another reason for not leaving the company.' Mr. L. writes, '. . . I belong to many clubs and associations because I think it is a good thing that other Swansea people see me at the right functions . . . I also belong to several social clubs as a duty really so that I meet the important Swansea people.'

Both emphasize the 'structure of opportunity', and how it differed for them. Mr. L. wrote, ' . . . it became obvious that I would follow my father . . .' He also stresses the relatively simple structure of his firm of wholesalers. Mr. T. writes of the complexity of his organization and the decisions to be made about whether to stay on the research side or to move over to the administrative side. This is perhaps best brought out when Mr. L. and Mr. T. discuss their future, as already pointed out Mr. L. presumes that he will stay in Swansea, but Mr. T. writes:

> There are five places I could move to from here, four in this country and one in Holland; three of those in this country are basically similar plants to the one at which I now work and I would only go to them as top man . . . I cannot make up my mind whether it is better to go to London and become really known and then become a local top man, then move back to London, or try to become a local top man first, moving to London later.

Mr. L. writes about his relationships with the locality, in which he is tied both economically and socially, whereas Mr. T. writes about his relationship to the organization for which he works, to which he is also tied, but not so strongly, economically and socially.

The two men also emphasize their educational backgrounds. This is another point that is developed later. Mr. L. writes, 'although I have no paper qualifications, I run the firm'. Mr. T.'s initial mobility was institutionalized through the educational system, grammar school, university followed by a period of research leading to a Ph.D.

These two career autobiographies are valuable research documents because they show what these two very different men thought of as important to their careers. However, case materials are a threat to the researcher, whose loving care to turn his matchless insights on every crumb of his findings may trip him into platitudes. These two case studies must be considered in the perspective of the quantitative sections that follow.

## 3 *The Mobility Quotient*

Both the estates studied were new (the oldest house was first occupied three and a half years before the fieldwork began) and so all the households had experienced some residential mobility, either locally or over a longer distance. The exceptions to this were twelve households that were first formed on the estates, at or shortly after marriage. Of the 108 longer established households, 38 had previously lived in Swansea (34 in the west, four in the east), 23 had previously lived elsewhere in Wales (18 in urban South Wales, two in urban North Wales and three in rural Wales), and 47 had previously lived outside Wales (41 in England, one in Scotland and five outside the United Kingdom).

A 'mobility quotient' was calculated to give an approximate numerical value to the geographical mobility experience of the households studied. This was based on the career mobility of the husbands in terms of the number of towns lived in, and on the number of years he had been in the labour force (excluding national service and war service unless he was a member of the regular forces, and excluding full-time further education). The necessity to control for age has been discussed in the earlier section on the middle class career pattern.

The formula used was:

$$50 - \frac{y}{x} = \text{mobility quotient. (m.q.)}$$

where $x$ = the number of towns lived in, $y$ = the number of years that the husband has been in the labour force. The result is taken away from 50 so that a high mobility quotient will mean a great deal of geographical mobility and not vice versa. 50 was chosen as it was thought to be the maximum number of years that one person would spend in the labour force; so that if someone spent the whole of his working life of 50 years in one town he would have a m.q. of 0. In the previous section Mr. L. who had spent all his working life of 21 years in Swansea has a m.q. of 29. Mr. T. who had spent his working life of between nine and ten years in four towns has a m.q. of 47·6. For example a headmaster who had lived in two towns of which Swansea was the second and had been teaching for 31 years would have a m.q. of 34·5 $(50 - \frac{31}{2})$; or a shop owner who had lived and worked in Swansea all his working life for 41 years would have a m.q. of 9 $(50 - \frac{41}{1})$. On the other hand an operations research engineer who had lived in three towns before Swansea and had been in the labour force for 14 years would have a m.q. of 46·5 $(50 - \frac{14}{3·5})$.

The table shows the distribution of mobility quotients for the 120 households studied.

TABLE 2:1

| Mobility quotient | Number of households |
|---|---|
| 50–49 | 4 |
| 48–47 | 22 |
| 46–45 | 16 |
| 44–43 | 19 |
| 42–41 | 15 |
| 40–39 | 9 |
| 38–37 | 8 |
| 36–35 | 5 |
| 34–33 | 5 |
| 32–31 | 3 |
| 30–29 | 5 |
| 28–27 | 3 |
| 26–25 | 1 |
| 24–23 | |
| 22–21 | |
| 20–19 | 1 |
| 18–17 | 2 |
| 16–15 | |
| 14–13 | 1 |
| 12–11 | 1 |
| 10–9 | |
| 8–7 | |
| 6–5 | |
| 4–3 | |
| 2–1 | |

Total 120

The arithmetic mean of these m.q.s is 39·925, there are 44 households with a lower m.q. than average, i.e. had experienced relatively little geographical mobility (on average they had lived in each town for at least ten years) and 76 households with higher than average m.q., i.e. had experienced considerable geographical mobility. However it should be noted that the high mobility quotients in the above table are a little misleading because they include those households with husbands who have only been in the labour force for a relatively short time. This fault can to a certain extent be corrected if the 20 households that have not experienced any geographical mobility are excluded from the table: for then only mobile households are included and as the mobility quotient is meant as a measure of mobility, this will then exclude those misleadingly included.

TABLE 2:2

| Mobility quotient | Number of households |
|---|---|
| 50–49 | 2 |
| 48–47 | 22 |
| 46–45 | 14 |
| 44–43 | 17 |
| 42–41 | 13 |
| 40–39 | 8 |
| 38–37 | 5 |
| 36–35 | 5 |
| 34–33 | 4 |
| 32–31 | 3 |
| 30–29 | 3 |
| 28–27 | 2 |
| 26–25 | 1 |
| 24–23 | |
| 22–21 | |
| 20–19 | |
| 18–17 | 1 |
| 16–15 | |
| 14–13 | |
| 12–11 | |
| 10–9 | |
| 8–7 | |
| 6–5 | |
| 4–3 | |
| 2–1 | |

Total 100

36

With the 20 immobile households excluded the preceding table shows the m.q. of the 100 mobile households.

The arithmetic mean is now 40·48 and there are 33 households below it even though they are non-locals who have experienced relatively little geographical mobility and 65 households with high mobility rates above it.

(Throughout this study when individuals are mentioned the m.q. for their household will be quoted as an indication of the amount of geographical mobility experienced.)

In addition to calculating past geographical mobility by the m.q. an attempt was also made to estimate potential geographical mobility. This is obviously a great deal more hazardous, especially as many had only just moved to the estate. Questions about potential mobility were often at first met with a vehement 'never again'—an opinion coloured by recent experiences of moving. But in fact less than half (54) of the households expected to be living on either estate in five years' time. For many households then, even though they had *all* moved to the estate recently, the estates were regarded as only a temporary place of residence. Those who expected to move should be divided between those who expected to move away from the estate but to stay within the locality and those who expected to move away from Swansea altogether. Both Mr. L. and Mr. T. expected to move away from the estate on which they now lived, but Mr. L. did not expect to move away from Swansea whereas Mr. T. did.

The estates then were regarded as temporary by two very different kinds of residents. There were those for whom the estate was one step in the Swansea housing ladder, e.g. a butcher (m.q. = 19) who used to live over his shop and as his business expanded had moved to the estate and now talked in terms of moving 'out to Gower or somewhere we can see the sea' in the next few years. He would not however leave Swansea. At the other extreme there was a civil engineer (m.q. = 47·5) who had come to South Wales to build a bridge and would leave the area altogether when it was completed. He knew that his time in Swansea and on the estate was very limited and almost from the day of his arrival began to think about where he would live next. This fundamental division between locals and non-locals which runs throughout this work can be illustrated by an examination of the reasons given for moving from the estate by the 66 households who expected so to do within five years. 44 of them specifically mentioned a change in the husbands' career pattern which would involve geographical mobility. Usually this also explicitly involved a promotion for the husband. The 22 who did not specifically mention the husband's career, mentioned variously a desire to live further in the country, or to get a bigger (and better) house, or an adjustment to stage change in the family cycle (i.e. either when they had children, or when their children left home). Usually this was seen as only involving relatively short distance residential mobility with the implicit assumption that the husband would continue to work at the same place.

Of the 44 households that expected to move away from the locality 42 were non-locals in the first place. Of the two locals who expected to become geographically mobile, one had gone to the local grammar school, and then to the local university college where he stayed on and obtained two research degrees and became a member of staff (m.q. $= 41$ which is high because he had only been in the labour force nine years). He expected to leave the area now and said 'it's about time I shook the dust of Swansea from my feet'. The other local (m.q. $= 33$) had recently broken with his partner and thought 'the town is not big enough for both of us'.

The 22 households who did not expect to move away from the locality, but did expect to move from the estate within five years were equally divided between locals and non-locals. For the locals, as mentioned above, the estate was seen as a step on the housing ladder. The eleven non-locals who expected to move from the estate but not from the locality had *all* moved straight to the estate when they came to Swansea and so can be said to be using the estates as a base while they are becoming established in the locality. They often had aims of 'cross-mobility' (Plowman, Minchinton and Stacey: 1962) but in the opposite direction to the term's original usage: they were attempting to enter the local social-system. (This point is elaborated later, especially in Chapter Seven.)

Very few of the 54 households that expected to remain on the estates for at least five years were locals, in fact only seven were, and for them their house on the estate was often at the top of their housing ladder. Two of these seven local households had moved to the estate on retirement, which was associated with their children leaving home: 'I wanted a smaller house that was easier to look after.' So of the 54 households that did not expect to move from the estate in the next five years 47 were non-locals, i.e. had been geographically mobile during the husband's career. Their character is hinted at by the fact that their m.q. is 35·5 compared to the average m.q. of 39·925 for all 120 households. This is a reflection of the greater number of years spent in the labour force.

They include the 31 households that Watson would have called 'blocked' spiralists: 'an older man . . . who reckons he has reached the last stage he can reasonably expect to achieve' (1960, p. 418). However it is analytically necessary to distinguish between those who had reached the top of their hierarchy and for whom there was nowhere else to move, and those who had decided they could go no further, because for example they either wished for no greater responsibility or they lacked the ability for greater responsibility. There is an obvious difference between a professor who has reached the top of the academic hierarchy and can only exchange his position for a similar one at the top of a similar hierarchy and a university lecturer who through inability or affection for a particular locality, cannot or will not move to a senior post in another university. The professor being in a 'bridging occupation' (Broom and Smith: 1963) it is possible for him to make a 'situs' change (Morris and Murphy: 1959) and to become for example a senior civil servant or full-time writer, but these situs changes I would expect to be relatively rare and certainly they did not occur within the families I studied.

18 of the 31 so-called 'blocked' spiralists thought they were at the top of their hierarchy and saw little point in moving their place of residence during the rest of their working lives, although some spoke in general terms of moving on retirement. For example a 47-year-old personnel manager of a large plant who had lived in three different localities before Swansea (m.q. = 42) said 'why should I move now, I can't get any higher, I can't get any more money without going to the States and I'm too old for that. No, we're going to settle—when my eldest leaves home and I retire we might buy a cottage in Hampshire (his home

county) but not for a long time certainly.' Similar remarks could be quoted from previously geographically mobile bank managers and teachers. They perhaps can be called 'achieved spiralists'. A bank manager (m.q. = 40) said he celebrated his decision not to move any more by buying fitted carpets which it had not been worthwhile to buy earlier in his career as he would have had to leave them behind when he moved on.

There were 13 'blocked' spiralists who admitted they were not at the top. As this is not an 'in-plant' study it is really impossible to say whether they had 'blocked themselves', so to speak by just not wanting to move, or were 'blocked' by their inability to go any higher. Dalton approaching managerial mobility from a different point of view of the industrial sociologist had similar difficulty with this problem. He wrote that 'the search for quantitative bulwarks often leads students to treat their admittedly indispensable factual data as terminal answers' (1959, p. 149), and concludes from the study of a single plant that 'age, work background and service, and formal education all showed such variation at Milo (the plant he studied) that none of them could regularly be formal tests for recruitment and promotion' (p. 167). In Tausky and Dubin's terminology 'blocked spiralists' tended to have a 'downward' career anchorage model and stressed how far they had come, rather than how far there was still to go to the top of the hierarchy. Often explicit in their apparent lack of further ambition was the realization that promotion would involve geographical mobility which in their eyes was undesirable. For example a 42-year-old 'shift' engineer (m.q. = 40·7) for whom promotion would have entailed moving to another plant elsewhere in Britain said:

> I've done alright, I started on the shopfloor, became foreman and went to night school. We've had to move around (Swansea was his third town) but now I'm satisfied. I like Swansea and the children are happy here. No, I won't move, probably ever, they only appoint above my level from outside, so I'll stick here, it's O.K. by me.

Of the 16 non-locals who did not expect to move from the estates two were retired, one a school teacher who although he was born and started his career outside the locality had worked in the town for 38 years (m.q. = 22), the other a retired shopkeeper had moved to the estate when he sold his shop. The latter said somewhat fatalistically 'I've always wanted to live near Gower and this'll do me until I die.'

Nine non-locals thought they might move sometime later during the husband's working life. They are of particular interest because unlike most of the households studied they did not have a particularly well developed sense of 'career'. One household in fact decided to move during the fieldwork having previously said that it was extremely unlikely that they would move for a long time. Typically this group had previously also been geographically mobile for 'non-career' reasons. E.g. A transport manager (m.q. = 44) who moved to Swansea to be closer to his parents who were becoming elderly: 'I took a drop in money but someone had to look after them and it was easier for us to move than it was for them, so we came. Might stay for ever, don't really know.' Another, a journalist (m.q. = 36) had changed his job to be near the sea: 'I've always wanted to live by the sea and so when I heard of the job I went after it—no it's not a promotion.' (Previously he worked for a national morning daily.)

Finally there were among the 47 non-local households who did not expect to move from the estate, five households that can be considered together. None of these five husbands could really be said to work for a bureaucratic hierarchy and all five were what is usually thought of as professional workers (one Dentist, one Architect, one Insurance Broker and two Chartered Accountants). They all had a high m.q., 47, 45, 48, 42, and 44, respectively, but this was really a reflection of the relatively short time they had been in the labour force. They had all moved to Swansea because of 'partnership' or 'practice' possibilities and all were becoming locals in that they thought it was very unlikely that they would ever leave the locality (i.e. 'cross-mobility'). They are very similar to the eleven non-locals who expected to leave the estate but not the locality, mentioned above.

Table 2:3 overleaf summarizes the main points in the data presented above.

The terminology that is used in this book is based on the six basic divisions in this table. The locals who are non-movers from the estate and/or the locality will be called the '*burgesses*': (after Watson 1964) 18 households in all (of which Mr. L. in section two is an example). The non-local, non-movers from

TABLE 2:3   *Potential Residential Mobility (in households)*

|  | *Non-movers from estates and locality within 5 yrs.* | *Movers from estates but not locality within 5 yrs.* | *Movers from estates and locality within 5 yrs.* | *Totals* |
|---|---|---|---|---|
| Locals | 7 | 11 | 2 | 20 |
| Non-Locals | 47 | 11 | 42 | 100 |
| Totals | 54 | 22 | 44 | 120 |
| Mobility quotient | 35·3 | 39·9 | 44·3 | mean = 39·925 |

the estate and/or the locality will be called '*spent spiralists*': 58 households (this will include the 13 true '*blocked spiralists*' and 18 '*achieved spiralists*'). Many of the spent spiralists will be more or less 'cross-mobile'. The non-local movers from the locality will be called the '*active spiralists*': 42 households (of which Mr. T. in section two is an example). And the local movers as the '*potential spiralists*': 2 households.

(This is of course moving away from Watson's original definitions because not all those I called 'spiralists' are working within a bureaucratic hierarchy. But they do all have the common feature of geographical mobility: either in the past, or the future.)

TABLE 2:4   *Non-Movers*

Summary of characteristics of those households who did not expect to move from either estate within the next 5 years.

| Locals: | | Total 7 |
|---|---|---|
| Retired | 2 | |
| Non-Locals: | | Total 47 |
| Retired | 2 | |
| 'Spent-spiralists': | 31 | |
| 'Blocked spiralists' | 13 | |
| 'Achieved spiralists' | 18 | |
| Cross-mobile professional | 5 | |
| 'Undecided, might move in the future' | 9 | |
| | | Total 54 |

A comparison of the average mobility quotient for each of these groups brings out the differences between them. The eighteen burgesses have an average m.q. of 34·5 (range 11–44); the spent spiralists have an average m.q. of 41·6 (range 36·1–46); the active spiralists have a m.q. average of 44·9 (range 41–49·3); the two potential spiralists have m.q.s of 41 and 33.

# CHAPTER THREE

# Social Mobility

## I  *Between Generations*

The relationship between geographical and social mobility amongst these families can now be analysed. Much depends however on the operationalizing of a definition of social mobility.

If social mobility is defined conventionally as movement from a manual occupation to a non-manual occupation intergenerationally the following two-way table can be produced:

TABLE 3:1  *Mobility*

|  | *Geographical mobility* | *Geographical immobility* |
|---|---|---|
| Socially Mobile | 31 | — |
| Socially Immobile | 69 | 20 |

As all the families studied were in non-manual occupations, by this definition none of them can have been downwardly socially mobile. Amongst these 120 families there were none that had been socially mobile without some, usually considerable geographical mobility, i.e. nobody came from a home in western Swansea where the principal breadwinner was in a manual occupation.

Continuing to define social mobility as intergenerational occupational change, increasing subtleties can be introduced by using a finer occupational classification than the manual/non-manual division, e.g. the Registrar-General's five 'social-classes' or even his 16 'socio-economic groups', or following Glass the Hall-Jones occupational classification. Their value is somewhat dubious for this study because of the possible unrepresentativeness of the families and the consequent futility of any elaborate juggling with the figures, especially as the total number of families studied was only 120. More importantly the previous studies of social mobility for example that of Glass *et al.* (1954) based on an occupational classification, do not achieve what they set out to do.

Once occupations receiving approximately the same rank are regarded as an *occupational class* and social status is defined in terms of occupation then the study of social stratification and social mobility is reduced to movements on an occupational scale. The general validity of any *single* occupational prestige scale by reference to which statuses may be allocated may be doubted. Not just the oft-quoted rural/urban dichotomy, but in terms of traditional and non-traditional systems (Stacey: 1960), or local and non-local systems (Stacey and Harris: 1965).

In urban areas people often employ occupation as a *provisional* basis for classifying one another in some sort of hierarchy. As Gellner has written 'bureaucracy is the kinship of modern man' (1964, p. 154). This has been widely interpreted as proof of the primacy of occupation and its economic correlates in social stratification. It is perhaps inevitable that those writers who most emphasize the value of occupation as an index of status in modern industrial societies most generally minimize the significance of other ascriptive criteria and classifications, e.g. 'race', language.

To reduce social stratification to a hierarchial occupational order, it is necessary to establish a social grading of occupations, then social mobility will be directly measurable as movements along this occupational ladder, either inter- or intra-generationally. But as Frankenburg has recently astutely observed with particular reference to Glass: '(His) methods and the nature of (his) material lead (him) to the categorization of static strata and the description of the structural framework in which mobility operates' (1966(*a*), p. 125), even though the stated aim was to describe a process.

Carlsson (1956) after one of the most penetrating analyses of the semantics of class and mobility writes, when it comes to the crunch of operationalizing his definition, that 'social mobility is understood to mean change of status between two generations and status is defined by means of occupation'. He then follows the primrose path of comparing the occupational status of a man with that of his father, and calls the result social mobility. This procedure also underlies the two major comparative studies of social mobility: that of Lipset and Bendix (1959) and S. M. Miller (1960), as well as that of Glass and his associates. Such a methodology has two further weaknesses besides these mentioned above. It presumes that which it seeks to investigate, that occupations indicate social status and hence that the occupational prestige scale defines the composition of social strata. However, the 'standard-ranking' of occupations ignored, for example, proprietors, rentiers, financiers and politicians. The occupational classification used by Glass has as its highest category, 'professional and high administrative'. Now this cannot really be assumed to represent the highest levels of British society. Nor can the seven occupation strata of the Hall/Jones classification be assumed to correspond to any socially recognized strata in Britain. If nothing else, 'community studies' have shown that (Williams: 1956, Stacey: 1960, Littlejohn: 1963). The standard classification ignores those not gainfully employed, e.g. the young, the old, housewives, students.

Secondly, and probably more seriously is that the Hall/Jones classification does not really refer to occupations as it purports to do but to organizational status (an individual's position in a given organization). The organizational model that underlies the classification is that of the large bureaucratic corporation with well defined administrative hierarchies and graduated supervisory roles. Above the status limits represented by the highest levels of such organizations are set the independent professionals who operate private practices and serve as consultants together with senior bureaucrats whose prominence and political status are thus recognized at the price of consistency of classification. Presumably the distinction intended in this scale between administrative and executive roles is that between co-ordination and direction, but this remains unclear.

Watson argued that 'occupational status is not a sufficient criterion by which persons can be ranged on a unilinear social scale. There is a qualitative difference between manual occupations on the one hand and professional, managerial and admini-strative occupations on the other' (1964, pp. 155–6). When I had classified all 120 households by both the Hall/Jones and the Registrar-General's scale I was very tempted to quote Merton who has written of a classification he once devised that it 'proved to be logically impeccable, empirically applicable and virtually sterile' (1957, p. 391).

Even within one side of the great divide between manual and non-manual occupations there are what Watson calls different 'fields' of social mobility (1964, pp. 155–6), what I would prefer to call the differing 'contexts' of social mobility. Individuals can rise or fall in terms of nation wide, or even international bureau-cratic hierarchies, not only industrial and productive but also educational, political, religious, etc.; or of local communities. They can be spiralists, or burgesses, or in Merton's (1957) ter-minology cosmopolitans or locals. Because of qualitative differ-ences in these contexts of social mobility, they are very difficult to compare by the conventional methodology outlined above.

With all the above kept in mind the following tables are pre-sented based on the Registrar-General's 16 socio-economic groups. The 120 households are classified by the current occu-pation of the husband or by the last occupation for the four retired households. Two (both full-time students) were un-classifiable.[1]

TABLE 3:2

| Registrar-General's Socio-economic group | Number of households |
|---|---|
| 1 | 57 |
| 2 | 13 |
| 3 | 15 |
| 4 | 26 |
| 5 | 2 |
| 6 | 5 |
| Total | 118 |

The 120 households are now compared with the occupation of

[1] It is necessary to write a note about these two full-time students. The first of them was a 'mature' student and his father had died leaving him a small business which he sold. The money that he gained from this, he used firstly to buy his present house and secondly to subsidize three years at university. The second was renting a house (the owner was doing an over-seas tour of duty). He was a research student and was in receipt of con-siderable extended family aid which allowed him to live on the estate. Both

the husband's father at the time of the informant's first job (or if his father died earlier, his occupation at the time of his death).

It is possible to designate all those with fathers to the right of the thick 'stepped' line in Table 3:3 as having been socially mobile (not including those in socio-economic groups 13: Farmers—employers and managers, 14: Farmers—own account and 16: members of the armed forces (in this particular case a high ranking officer—eight in all) 66 households out of the total 120. This is obviously far from satisfactory because it excludes for example the 15 households where the father of the husband was an employer or manager in industry and commerce, in an establishment employing less than 25 persons, or the three households where the husband's father was a self employed professional worker.

TABLE 3:3 *in households.*

HUSBAND'S FATHERS' SOCIO–ECONOMIC GROUP

| Husbands socio-economic group | 1 | 2 | 3 | 4 | 5 | 6 | 7 | 8 | 9 | 10 | 11 | 12 | 13 | 14 | 15 | 16 | |
|---|---|---|---|---|---|---|---|---|---|---|---|---|---|---|---|---|---|
| 1 | 12 | 15 | 2 | 4 | 2 | 4 | 1 | 9 | 4 | | 2 | | 2 | | | | 57 |
| 2 | 1 | 7 | 1 | | 1 | 1 | | | 2 | | | | | | | | 13 |
| 3 | 3 | | 5 | 1 | 1 | | | 1 | | 2 | | | | 2 | | | 15 |
| 4 | 4 | 1 | 2 | 5 | 1 | 1 | 1 | 1 | 2 | | 4 | | | 3 | 1 | 1 | 26 |
| 5 | 1 | | | | | | | | | | 1 | | | | | | 2 |
| 6 | | 2 | | | 3 | | | | | | | | | | | | 5 |
| Totals | 21 | 25 | 10 | 10 | 8 | 6 | 2 | 12 | 6 | 6 | 3 | | 2 | 5 | 1 | 1 | 118 |
| Full time student | 1 | | | | | | | | | | 1 | | | | | | 120 |

non–manual (+ groups 13,14 & 16 89 households | Manual (minus groups 13,14 & 16 31 households

students were married. In the analysis I have treated the university as if it was their employer and in Chapter Nine where employers are classified, in terms of size, being a student is treated as if it was a job.

48

If however the table is converted to make use of the manual/ non-manual division then all those to the right of the thick straight line (with the above mentioned exceptions) have been socially mobile (31 households) and those to the left have not (89 households). A close examination of this table, especially of the 31 so-called socially mobile households shows that the largest group of socially mobile households come from homes where the husband's father was a foreman or supervisor, twelve households. If to these twelve the seven skilled manual workers are added this will leave only twelve households who have been socially mobile over any distance.

This does of course accord very closely to the findings of the macro-studies of social mobility which are mentioned above that the bulk of intergenerational social mobility is over a very short distance (B. G. Stacey: 1967, Glass: 1954).

## 2 *Education and Mobility*

There is a great deal of evidence to suggest that the educational system is a very important agent in the process of intergenerational mobility (e.g. D. V. Glass *et al.* (1954), especially the chapters by Floud, Himmelweit, and Hall and Glass; Floud, Halsey and Martin (1957)). Indeed it has been frequently argued that institutionalized *inter*generational mobility through the educational system makes *intra*generational mobility through the occupational system increasingly unlikely.

The importance of education in the mobility of Mr. T. in Chapter Two has already been discussed. In this section the educational experience of all 120 husbands studied is related to the variables discussed previously, geographical mobility and intergenerational social mobility.

The educational experience of the households studied varied widely, from having left school at 14 and never having been near an educational institution again, to having left school at 19, gone on to several universities and finishing with a doctorate. There are however certain broad relationships that can be shown between education and social and geographical mobility. The basic facts are summarized in the tables that follow below, building on the material that has gone before.

TABLE 3:4

| Husband's age at leaving school | Number |
|---|---|
| 14 | 4 |
| 15 | 8 |
| 16 | 30 |
| 17 | 22 |
| 18+ | 56 |
| | Total 120 |

Arithmetic mean = 16·96 years.

The arithmetic mean of the school leaving age of the husbands varies interestingly with the three major groups that the households have been divided into:

TABLE 3:5

| | |
|---|---|
| Socially and geographically immobile | 16·3 |
| Socially immobile and geographically mobile | 17·2 |
| Socially and geographically mobile | 17·5 |

The third table considers the type of school attended by the 120 husbands.

TABLE 3:6

| Type of school | Number |
|---|---|
| Major Public School | 5 |
| Minor Public School | 15 |
| State Grammar School | 79 |
| State 'Secondary Modern' | 12 |
| Other Secondary | 4 |
| Other (abroad) | 5 |
| | Total 120 |

*All* those who have been called socially mobile went to a state grammar school, like Mr. T. None of the socially and geographically immobile went to a major public school but seven attended a minor public school, the remaining 13 all attended the local grammar school, like Mr. M. The most heterogeneous group were the socially immobile but geographically mobile group, which was as follows:

TABLE 3:7

| Type of school | Number |
|---|---|
| Major Public School | 5 |
| Minor Public School | 8 |
| State Grammar School | 35 |
| State Secondary | 12 |
| Other Secondary | 4 |
| Abroad | 5 |
| Total | 69 |

In terms of the formal qualifications gained at school, 29 out of the 31 socially mobile husbands have 'A' levels or their equivalent, compared with only six of the 20 non-mobile husbands. 35 of the 69 geographically mobile and socially immobile husbands gained the equivalent of 'A' levels.

My data on education and mobility confirm the argument that the English school system is divided into two sets, one having little to do with mobility, but much do to with elite status while the other (the State system) has much to do with mobility and little to do with the recruitment of elites except for a tiny handful who achieve eminence in professional or public life after a prolonged competitive struggle through the universities and beyond (Halsey: 1961, p. 454).

The next table summarizes the data about formal education after leaving school for the 120 husbands studied and underlines the broad association between educational achievement, and social and geographical mobility. 23 of the 31 socially mobile husbands had spent at least a year full-time in a formal educational institution, compared to only four of the 20 locals (and two of these I have called 'potential spiralists' because they expect to become geographically mobile). All of the 31 socially mobile husbands had at least some formal education, if only part time since leaving school. Altogether there were 33 husbands who did not attend an educational institution at all after leaving school, none of them were in the group that had been socially and geographically mobile.

These data suggest very strongly the importance of formal educational qualifications as an aid to social mobility for those from manual backgrounds. Compare for example the figures for obtaining 'on the job' qualifications: none of those who had been socially mobile but 19 of those from middle class

E

TABLE 3:8

|  | Socially and geographically immobile | Socially immobile and geographically mobile | Socially and geographically mobile | Totals |
|---|---|---|---|---|
| University | 4 | 25 | 20 | 49 |
| Other full-time | — | 4 | 5 | 9 |
| Part-time only | 6 | 17 | 6 | 29 |
| 'On-job' only | 3 | 19 | — | 22 |
| None | 7 | 4 | — | 11 |
| Totals | 20 | 69 | 31 | 120 |

backgrounds. By 'on the job' is meant the kind of middle class apprenticeship typified by 'managerial trainees' and articled clerks in solicitors' offices. From these data, this kind of qualification seems to be more open to those from a middle class background than to those from a working class background. Those who have been socially mobile seemed to have first obtained a 'paper' qualification and then to have entered the occupation of their choice.

This point can be emphasized by comparing the mean number of years of all formal education after 16 of those husbands who have been socially mobile with those from middle class backgrounds:

TABLE 3:9 *Mean number of years of all formal education after age 16*

|  | Number | Mean | Range |
|---|---|---|---|
| Socially and geographically immobile | 20 | 2·1 | 0–6 |
| Socially immobile and geographically mobile | 69 | 4·3 | 0–9 |
| Socially and geographically mobile | 31 | 5·3 | 2–10 |

The following generalizations can therefore be made. The socially mobile group have not really been more geographically mobile than the socially immobile but geographically mobile group. (The former having a mean m.q. of 42·5 compared to 43 for the latter.) Although geographical mobility seems to be necessary for social mobility, together with formal educational qualifications, many households seem to have to be geographically mobile to maintain their position—even though they came from a middle class background. This is a reflection of the nature of the middle class career pattern, which is accepted as the 'supreme reality' for most members of the middle class and for many it entails geographical mobility, which must be accepted as part of the career.

The importance of education has been rightly stressed in many previous studies of social mobility but it would appear from these data that educational qualifications are also important (but not so important) for those from middle class backgrounds in maintaining their middle class position.

Against both these two groups must be seen the locals, the burgesses, those from middle class backgrounds in western Swansea, who, compared with the other 100 families studied have been far less mobile, either geographically or socially and do not have the same 'paper' qualifications. Whyte in *The Organization Man* found that 'the educational level is higher among the migrants than the non-migrants and the higher the educational level, the more intensive the migration' (1956, p. 248). My data agree with this finding. In a consideration of why the locals are so different it is necessary to move from general considerations of intergenerational social mobility, as is usually studied, to a more detailed consideration in differences of intragenerational social mobility, career mobility. This will be done in the next section. How much or how little geographical mobility it has entailed in the past, or may be expected to entail in the future has already been discussed in the previous chapter.

To conclude this section I would like to present a case study showing the inter-relationships between social and geographical mobility and education.

Living on the larger of the two estates were two non-locals from the same small west country town. One Mr. K. had been socially mobile, his father had been an agricultural labourer, and he was now a cost accountant for a light engineering factory. He had gone to the local grammar school and then to a provincial university where he had read mathematics. He had joined a very large organization after leaving university and had taken professional examinations. After four years he left this organization and moved to the Midlands to another company who two years later offered him his present job in South Wales where they were going to occupy a newly built factory. Mr. K. had been in Swansea one year when the fieldwork began (m.q. $= 47.7$) and anticipated remaining in South Wales for between three or four years when 'I'll get restless and want to be going on'.

Living on the same estate a few doors away was the man from the same town who by the definitions used previously had been geographically but not socially mobile, Mr. B. His father had been a very wealthy auctioneer/surveyor/estate agent in this town and B. had been sent away to a major public school. But as boys they had known each other, playing together when they were small. He had gone on to Oxford and when he came down he joined a large metallurgical concern working in their London 'front' offices. After three years he moved to South Wales to work on 'the managerial side' in the plant itself. He first lived elsewhere in South Wales moving to the present estate after eighteen months and had been living there two years when the fieldwork began (m.q. $= 47.5$). He did not think that he was likely to spend the rest of his career with the same firm or in South Wales and to my knowledge was actively looking for other jobs in the press. ('With my background I should be able to get something.')

Naturally enough they were both amazed to find each other neighbours, so far from home. They had been at university at almost the same time but had not associated during vacations. Mr. B. to me played down at first their previous social distance, saying only that Mr. K.'s father 'had worked on a farm', but Mr. K. said that although they had played as small children, B. as a teenager was not allowed to play with the village boys. Mr. K. said that Mr. B.'s father was 'proper gentry'—he rode to hounds and both his brother and his father (Mr. B.'s grandfather) owned 'hundreds of acres'.

On the estate they were quite friendly but did not see all that much of each other, however both mentioned the other first to me when I asked 'Who are you friendly with on the estate?' Their wives were more friendly and often dropped in on each other without warning (the definition that I used for a 'neighbour'). Both husbands emphasized the coincidence of their present common geographical location far more than the virtual abolition of the social distance in the past between their parents' families.

However there was one occasion that emphasized that social as well as geographical distance had been travelled by Mr. K. Mr. B.'s father was now dead and Mr. B.'s mother was visiting her son. Whilst she was there Mrs. K. dropped in, as was her practice on the way to the shops. She was introduced by Mrs. B. to B.'s mother and all was very polite. (Mrs. K. thought it was 'a bit strained'.) After she left B.'s mother complained to B.'s wife that she 'did not know what things were coming to when the wife of a son of a man in the village could call, without being invited, at her son's house—did it happen often?' From then on it was always carefully stage-managed that B.'s mother did not actually meet Mr. and Mrs. K.

K.'s social mobility through the educational system and consequent geographical mobility had allowed him to become a physical neighbour of B.'s and far more than this, their wives thought of each other as 'neighbours'. As yet it seemed that they had not been back to their mutual home town at the same time, but both said, when I asked, that it would be very difficult for them to go for a drink with each other. It then came out that K.'s brother was a farm labourer on B.'s brother's farm. B. said 'I couldn't go to the pub with him, because we don't go to the village pub, and besides if I did I would most likely go with my brother and he (Mr. K.) would be there with his brother and my brother is his brother's boss. Wouldn't be fair on anyone.' In Swansea Mr. K. and Mr. B. can and have been to a pub together.

## 3   *Work-life Mobility*

Besides the differences in past and potential geographical mobility, it has been shown that another major difference between locals and non-locals was in formal educational qualifications and as a consequent reflection of this, the differing ages at which they started work. These differences however do not stop here, in fact all the above differences between locals and non-locals are but symptoms of their differing contexts of social mobility: the local community or the occupation hierarchy. There is a marked contrast between the occupational context of locals and non-locals, illustrated by the contrast between Mr. L. and Mr. T.

Occupational contexts may be thought of as a continuum from a one-man business, with one branch employing only a boy and so with only one level of authority at one end, to a large international bureaucracy employing many thousands of people in many hundreds of branches and with many levels of authority at the other. The middle class career is worked out in many different contexts but it would be possible to fit most of them somewhere on this continuum in terms of these variables (size, number of branches, number and nature of levels of hierarchical authority). Although there was a wide range of career contexts among the 120 husbands studied—in fact as wide as the opposite ends of the continuum suggested above—there was a marked tendency for the 'locals' to be working at the 'smaller' end of the continuum and the non-locals to be working at the 'larger' end. The career autobiographies of Mr. L. and Mr. T both illustrate this point. It will be remembered that Mr. L.'s wholesaling firm was relatively simple in organization whereas that of Mr. T. was extremely complex and that of Mr. L. was completely local whereas that of Mr. T. was international.

The following tables bring out these points. Firstly by the total size of the organization for which they work, the locals and non-locals may be divided in the following way.

TABLE 3:10

| *Size of firm* | *Locals* | *Non-Locals* | *Total* |
|---|---|---|---|
| −25 employees | 5 | 7 | 12 |
| 25–500 employees | 9 | 28 | 37 |
| +500 employees | 1 | 54 | 55 |
| Self-employed professionals | 5 | 11 | 16 |
| Total | 20 | 100 | 120 |

This marked difference in occupational context between locals and non-locals can also be seen in the number of branches that the firm they work for has.

TABLE 3:11

| Number of branches of firm | Locals | Non-Locals | Total |
|---|---|---|---|
| 1 | 15 | 31 | 46 |
| 2 | 2 | 7 | 9 |
| 3–5 | 1 | 5 | 6 |
| 6–9 | — | 14 | 14 |
| 10–49 | 1 | 21 | 22 |
| 50–99 | 1 | 18 | 19 |
| 100+ | — | 4 | 4 |
| Totals | 20 | 100 | 120 |

The relationship between the size of the firm, the number of branches that it has, and geographical mobility can be shown by calculating the mean mobility quotient for each category in Tables 3:12 and 3:13 overleaf. Put simply, these findings mean that the larger the firm for whom one works and the more branches that it has, the more likely the employees are to have been geographically mobile. As the tables show, there is not always a direct and close correspondence but even with such an unrepresentative sample as this the tendency is clear.

Questions were asked about the number of levels of authority and about the bureaucratic hierarchy of the firm worked for. Although no difficulty was experienced in obtaining information about the overall size of their firm and the approximate number of branches, there was a general reluctance to give direct details about the internal organization of their firm. Consequently, as this proved to be a 'sensitive' subject it could not be pursued as systematically as would have been liked. Enough information was gathered indirectly, however, to be able to make certain generalizations about the nature and structure of the firms for which the 120 husbands work and to be able to draw out the

TABLE 3:12

| Size of firm | Locals m.q. | Non-Locals m.q. | Average m.q. |
|---|---|---|---|
| −25 employees | 32·5 | 41·3 | 36·9 |
| 25–500 employees | 35 | 42·1 | 38·5 |
| +500 employees | 40 | 45·1 | 42·3 |
| Self-employed professionals | 39 | 36 | 37·5 |
| Average m.q. | 36·6 | 43·3 | 39·9 |

TABLE 3:13

| No. of branches of firm | Locals m.q. | Non-Locals m.q. | Average m.q. |
|---|---|---|---|
| 1 | 32·1 | 36·2 | 34·4 |
| 2 | 29·1 | 38·9 | 34 |
| 3–5 | | 40·3 | 40·3 |
| 6–9 | | 45·3 | 45·3 |
| 10+ | 43·4 | 47·4 | 44·9 |
| 50+ | 42·1 | 47·3 | 49 |
| 100+ | | 48·3 | 48·3 |
| Average m.g. | 36·6 | 43·3 | 39·9 |

basic differences between the locals and the non-locals.

Here some data will be presented that perhaps should come in the next chapters: that on the middle class extended family. All 120 husbands were asked two questions about kin and occupations:

1. Is there any relative of yours working in the same firm as yourself?
2. Did a relative in *any way* help you get your job?

To the first question the answers were:

TABLE 3:14

|  | Locals | Non-Locals | Totals |
|---|---|---|---|
| Yes | 12 | 21 | 33 |
| No | 8 | 79 | 87 |
| Totals | 20 | 100 | 120 |

Of the twelve locals who replied in the affirmative eleven worked very closely with at least one relative like Mr. L. in Chapter Two (the twelfth in fact worked in a distant town). Of the 21 non-locals who worked in the same firm as at least one other relative only four were working at all closely. Typical of the other 17 was an I.C.I. man who had a brother-in-law who worked in an I.C.I. plant in Scotland, but not even in the same division of I.C.I.

Paralleling the closeness of the locals' working relationship with their kinsmen was their closeness genealogically, and vice versa for the non-locals. The eleven locals who worked with at least one relative worked respectively with:

> 4 fathers
> 2 fathers-in-law
> 3 brothers
> 1 brother-in-law
> 1 son

This can be compared with the 4 non-locals who worked closely with:

> 1 brother-in-law
> 1 step-sister's son
> 1 cousin (mother's sister's son)
> 1 'cousin' (for whom it was impossible to work
>        out a more exact relationship)

To the eleven locals mentioned above should be added two others who once worked very closely with a now deceased father. These 13 all in fact worked in what are usually considered to be 'family businesses', that did not spread their interests far outside the locality even if they had more than one

59

branch. They were often truly tied economically to the locality, dependent upon a business that had been built up over two or three generations. The largest of these family businesses employed over 400 people but was tied to the locality. The 'son' who lived on one of these estates when asked about potential geographical mobility said 'I could as easily leave Swansea as fly'—graphically illustrating the difference between himself and his neighbour who had worked out on a piece of paper which branches of his firm he would be likely to move to next if he stayed on the 'technical' side and which he was likely to be moved to if he moved over to the 'administrative' side, also working out how long he would have to stay at various future branches, as well as how long he was likely to stay in Swansea. These are very similar to the cases of Mr. L. and Mr. T., but in fact refer to different people.

To the second question, 'Did any relative in any way help you get your job?' the answers were:

TABLE 3:15

|  | Locals | Non-Locals | Totals |
|---|---|---|---|
| Yes | 14 | 4 | 18 |
| No | 6 | 96 | 102 |
| Totals | 20 | 100 | 120 |

As mentioned above 13 of the locals work in family businesses and so this question really is a little superfluous—the fourteenth local obtained a job in a firm of chartered accountants through the good offices of his maternal grandfather.

It is likely that the number of non-locals who received *any* help from a relative is likely here to be somewhat understated. For the locals who often were working in family businesses it was very difficult to deny, but for those who have been geographically mobile denial can be more easily facilitated. Throughout the fieldwork I found that where aid amongst kin was being considered, that while it was thought to be a 'bad thing' to receive aid, universally they themselves gave aid—in terms of advice or more materially (compare Hubert 1965). 'To give is better than to receive.' (This point is developed in the next chapter.) It is certain that when compared to the locals, the non-locals were far less likely to work with a close kinsman and probably far less likely to have got their job in the first place through a kinsman.

This section has given some quantification to specific points raised in the two career autobiographies in Chapter Two. The data about the size of firms and the number of kin working in them are good indicators of the differing contexts of social mobility of middle class families.

## 4 *Friends and Mobility*

Chapters Two and Three are seen primarily as presenting the facts of social and geographical mobility as experienced by the 120 households studied. This section however is more akin to the later chapters of the book, where the effects of this mobility are analysed. This chapter deals very generally with friends and mobility and some of the points that it raises will be returned to later, especially in the discussions of neighbourhood relationships.

During the original door-to-door survey on the two estates questions were asked about friends. I did not specify what I meant by friendship hoping that it would later emerge what they themselves thought about friends and friendships. Data

TABLE 3:16

| Best friends last seen | Husbands | Wives | Total |
|---|---|---|---|
| Within last 24 hours | 2 | 9 | 11 |
| Within last week | 11 | 23 | 34 |
| Within last month | 33 | 31 | 64 |
| Within last year | 41 | 34 | 75 |
| Longer | 21 | 17 | 38 |
| 'Don't have one' | 12 | 6 | 18 |
| Total | 120 | 120 | 240 |
| Telephoned in last month | 11 | 31 | 42 |
| Written to in last month | 25 | 42 | 67 |

were systematically and uniformly collected about both husbands' and wives' 'best friends': when they were last seen, where they lived, how they were first met and their occupation (or that of their husbands). To the question, When did you last see your best friend? the replies given in Table 3:16 were obtained (see previous page).

Obvious reservations must be made about this table because it was not possible to ask everybody on the same day, consequently some will have been asked just after a weekend which tended to inflate the amount of contact and perhaps more importantly, the field work was begun just after Christmas and so I would expect the number seen 'within the last month' also to be somewhat inflated. However, there is no reason to anticipate that these possible distortions are not randomly distributed between locals and non-locals and so the data are still valuable for a comparison between them.

TABLE 3:17

| Best friends last seen | Locals | | | | Non-Locals | | Totals |
| --- | --- | --- | --- | --- | --- | --- | --- |
| | Husbands | | Wives | | Husbands | Wives | |
| | % | n | % | n | n & % | n & % | n |
| Within last 24 hours | 10 | 2 | 35 | 7 | — | 2 | 11 |
| Within last week | 40 | 8 | 35 | 7 | 3 | 16 | 34 |
| Within last month | 30 | 6 | 25 | 5 | 27 | 26 | 64 |
| Within last year | 5 | 1 | — | — | 40 | 34 | 75 |
| Longer | 5 | 1 | — | — | 20 | 17 | 38 |
| 'Don't have one' | 10 | 2 | 5 | 1 | 10 | 5 | 18 |
| Total | 100 | 20 | 100 | 20 | 100 | 100 | 240 |
| Telephone in last month | | 2 | | 15 | 9 | 16 | 42 |
| Written to in last week | | 1 | | 7 | 24 | 35 | 67 |

The above results were not of course unexpected and are largely self-explanatory. There is however a difference in the use of telephoning and letter writing to best friends between locals and non-locals. This is partially explained by the next table which shows that the locals tend to live nearer their best friends and so there is not as great a need to write to them. The similarity in the use of the telephone by wives is in spite of the different purpose for which the telephone is being used: by the locals, either for a gossip or to arrange an imminent meeting and by the non-locals for more important news. The crude measure of having telephoned in 'the last month' masks the fact that the locals in fact telephone their friends far more often than do non-locals.

Before too much significance is attached to the figures in Table 3:17 it would be as well to examine very closely the geographical location of 'best friends' of locals and non-locals. When this is done (below) it will be seen that this goes some way towards accounting for the difference between locals' and non-locals' contact rates with their best friends.

TABLE 3:18

| *Location of best friend* | *Locals* | | *Non-Locals* | | *Totals* |
|---|---|---|---|---|---|
| | *Husbands* | *Wives* | *Husbands* | *Wives* | |
| | % n | % n | n & % | n & % | n |
| Western Swansea | 65 13 | 75 15 | 2 | 6 | 36 |
| Eastern Swansea | — — | 5 1 | — | — | 1 |
| Within 25 miles | 15 3 | 10 2 | 11 | 14 | 30 |
| Within 100 miles | 5 1 | 5 1 | 24 | 20 | 46 |
| Over 100 miles | — — | — — | 47 | 48 | 95 |
| Abroad | 5 1 | — — | 6 | 7 | 14 |
| 'Don't have one' | 10 2 | 5 1 | 10 | 5 | 18 |
| Total | 100 20 | 100 20 | 100 | 100 | 240 |

The key figures above are for those living over 100 miles away —none of the locals have 'best-friends' living in this country over 100 miles away, but almost half of the non-locals 'best-friends' are that distance away. The data presented in the above table has important consequences for social relationships on the estate, because as will be shown in Chapters Six and Seven of this book non-locals are far more dependent upon the estate for day-to-day contacts and friendship than are the locals. The locals continue their extra-estate friendships and often have local kin as well. On the other hand non-locals especially those who have moved to the locality recently have neither local extra-estate friends nor local kin and so tend to rely far more on their geographical neighbours.

All those designated 'best friends' by the 89 households that came from non-manual backgrounds were either in non-manual jobs or married to husbands in non-manual jobs. This however is not so for the 31 households that come from a working class background. (N.B. all socially mobile households have also been geographically mobile.)

TABLE 3:19

| Occupation of 'best friends' of socially mobile households | Husbands | Wives | Totals |
|---|---|---|---|
| Manual occupation | 6 | 2 | 8 |
| Non-manual occupation | 18 | 25 | 43 |
| 'Don't have one' | 7 | 4 | 11 |
| Total | 31 | 31 | 62 |

Firstly it should be noticed that of the total of 18 individuals who said they did not have a 'best friend', eleven were from socially mobile households. Secondly only eight of the socially mobile households claimed as a 'best friend' someone who might be called working class. These eight were seen very infrequently and none had been seen in the last month. Further significant contrasts can be drawn between locals and non-locals when considering how 'best friends' were first met. Firstly the combined totals (see Table 3:20).

This table is again self-explanatory but there are one or two points about it that need to be brought out. The large number of wives' 'best friends' that were first met through husbands. This is in accord with what little research has been done on the subject in North America. A paper entitled 'The primary relations of middle class couples' (Babchuk and Bates: 1963) was subtitled 'a study in male dominance'. It shows (from a sample of 39 couples) that the husband had the greater

TABLE 3:20

| Where first met | Husband | Wife | Total |
|---|---|---|---|
| Childhood (incl. school) | 26 | 17 | 43 |
| College/university | 16 | 8 | 24 |
| Club/society/association/ church | 5 | 11 | 16 |
| Work | 31 | 16 | 47 |
| Ex-neighbours | 18 | 19 | 37 |
| Present neighbours | 1 | 9 | 10 |
| Other (incl. 'don't know') | 5 | 7 | 12 |
| Through wife | 4 | — | 4 |
| Through husband | — | 21 | 21 |
| Through other relative | 2 | 6 | 8 |
| 'Don't have one' | 12 | 6 | 18 |
| Totals | 120 | 120 | 240 |

influence in initiating friendships and in determining who the 'best friends' of the couple will be.

This point can be developed if locals are contrasted with non-locals on how best friends were first met (Table 3:21). This

TABLE 3:21

| Where first met | Locals | | Non-Locals | | Totals |
|---|---|---|---|---|---|
| | Husbands | Wives | Husbands | Wives | |
| Childhood (incl. school) | 12 | 10 | 14 | 7 | 43 |
| College/university | 1 | 1 | 15 | 7 | 24 |
| Club/association/ society/church | 2 | 2 | 3 | 9 | 16 |
| Work | — | 1 | 31 | 15 | 47 |
| Ex-neighbour | 1 | 1 | 17 | 18 | 37 |
| Present neighbour | — | — | 1 | 9 | 10 |
| Other (incl. 'don't know') | — | — | 5 | 7 | 12 |
| Through wife | 1 | — | 3 | — | 4 |
| Through husband | — | 4 | — | 17 | 21 |
| Through other relative | 1 | — | 1 | 6 | 8 |
| 'Don't have one' | 2 | 1 | 10 | 5 | 18 |
| Totals | 20 | 20 | 100 | 100 | 240 |

shows that the 'male dominance' is more marked for the latter than for the former. This table underlines the importance of 'work' as a source of 'best friends' for the geographically mobile when compared with the non-mobile. Also as a reflection of their mobility the non-locals claim far more ex-neighbours, 35, than the locals. It will be remembered that Mr. T. thought of his colleagues as his friends.

Babchuk and Bates in their above-mentioned paper use the concept of a 'suspended primary group' for the friendship groups of geographically mobile members of the North American middle class. These friendships can be reactivated at either very short notice or with a change in the location of the friends. To illustrate the nature of 'suspended primary groups' I will give two examples of long distance friendships of geographically mobile households; the second had been socially mobile as well.

Firstly a 52-year-old senior civil servant for whom Swansea was his seventh town (m.q. = 46) and so had been very mobile geographically. Both he and his wife gave as their best friends another couple who lived in the north of England—the husband was in a very similar occupation and had been equally mobile. Although they wrote to each other regularly approximately once a month they only actually saw each other once a year when they always went on holiday with each other for three weeks, usually abroad. By any measure of geographical distance or of 'contact' they were far from close and yet it was obviously an extremely important and close relationship.

Secondly and perhaps more interestingly is the case of a friendship network of a 34-year-old insurance man (m.q. = 45·3). He had been both socially and geographically mobile and gave as his best friend someone he had met at school who now lived abroad. They had not seen each other for over five years, and the same can be said of the other four old school friends with whom he kept in touch (they had a complicated mechanism for doing so: Individual A wrote to individual B who read A's letter and wrote one of his own and posted both to C, who did the same posting all three letters to D. And so on until F posted all six letters back to A, who took out his old and five times read letter and wrote a new one which he posted with the other five to B, and so on round again and again). They very rarely met but I was assured that if they were ever in the same part of the country they would. This is a particularly fine example of a 'suspended primary group'.

In both these cases, because of geographical mobility the friendship was situationally dormant for most of the time but to the individuals concerned it represented a subjectively vital relationship. There is of course a very strong parallel that can be drawn with the relationships between geographically scattered kin (see next chapter). The locals in contrast saw their 'best friends' very frequently compared to the non-locals and so, as with kin, any crude measure of 'contact' which ignores the distance factor is not very meaningful.

To assess the real differences in social relations between those members of the middle class who have been geographically mobile and those who have not, and those who have been socially mobile and those who have not, it is necessary to look in detail at the strategic institution of the family.

# CHAPTER FOUR

# The Middle Class Extended Family

## I  *Introduction*

It is difficult to write about the middle class family when one either comes from such a family or is procreating one. But I hope to illustrate some aspects of the structure and function of the family, which even if part of general experience do not seem to be part of the literature; and to rise above the anecdotal and make some contribution to a discussion of the structure and function of the family in modern society.

I must at once limit the field; as the material presented was collected during a study of social and geographical mobility attention will be concentrated on those aspects that are particularly relevant to these themes. I am not for example going to deal with socialization processes or with all the advantages of the middle class home environment in exploiting the educational system (see B. G. Stacey: 1965). I make therefore no pretence that this is an exhaustive analysis of the structure and function of the middle class family.

In short, I am going to suggest that the middle class extended family has functions that are relevant to a study of social mobility: functions that are often ignored by the overwhelming concentration on the occupation/status dimension of social mobility; and that an examination of these functions will enable certain aspects of the structure of the extended family, that have hitherto been somewhat overshadowed by the emphasis on the mother/married daughter link, to become apparent.

This is an attempt at synthesis between two disparate fields of sociology; that of the family and kin, and that of social mobility. In examining the inter-relationships between these two social systems, that of the family and that of class, it is important not to over-emphasize one at the expense of the other. As for example did Lloyd Warner when he made a 'sponge-word' out of status (cf. C. Wright Mills: 1942). In most analyses it is important to keep different systems separate, but here an attempt is deliberately made at synthesis. With notable exceptions this synthesis has not been attempted before and so the previous literature in both fields is only rarely very helpful. I will however summarize the more relevant findings.

Raymond Firth perhaps has best put the position of kinship in Britain: 'pervasive, intangible, still largely unstudied with its significance either not appreciated or in danger of being overemphasized' (1961, p. 305). In attempting to study some aspects of kinship in an area where its significance is often not appreciated I hope that I will not overemphasize it. As Rosser and Harris concluded after a major study 'Kinship is essentially a minor matter in the structure of urban Swansea, if important in the lives of individuals' (1965, p. 287).

I must make quite clear what I mean by the term 'extended family'. I am going to follow Rosser and Harris who after reviewing the previous literature define the 'extended family' as 'any persistent kinship grouping of persons related by descent, marriage or adoption, which is wider than the elementary family, in that it characteristically spans three generations from grandparents to grandchildren' (1965, p. 32). Their definition concentrates attention on the extended family as a social entity and leaves its actual form under varying conditions to be determined by analysis. I am here attempting to determine its form for the urban middle class who have varied experiences of geographical and social mobility.

The previous work on kin and the family in Britain has not often been directly concerned with the effects of mobility. Although its importance has been recognized for example by Lorraine Lancaster, who included it in a list of twelve variables relevant to kin studies (1961, p. 319).[1] J. B. Loudon

---

[1] The 12 listed variables being: 1. total range of kin recognition; 2. composition of households; 3. cycle of development of the nuclear family;

in a companion paper similarly would want to include social mobility, along with physical mobility, occupation, economic resources, ownership of property, religious affiliation and level of education as being relevant to any study of kinship behaviour (1961, p. 337).

As earlier pointed out (see Introduction), I make no claim for the *statistical* validity of this study, although later I compare in detail the geographical distribution of, and contact between members of the extended family with other studies, and I have followed the view taken by Lorraine Lancaster in the above mentioned paper that the relatedness of the factors relevant to kin studies, 'is easier to show descriptively (and perhaps to discover) in an intensive study where the complexity of social facts in any particular situation comes out clearly'. Also 'intensive research is likely to remain useful in providing evidence for the content of relationships'. And 'qualitative observational methods may provide the only basis to go on in estimating the strength, nature and ideological backing of relationships' (1961, p. 319).

I collected complete genealogies for 32 of the 120 families. I have found that their direct value in proportion to the time they took to collect was small. Especially as this was not primarily a study of kinship. As Loudon has written, 'While the number of kin with whom an individual may have some kind of periodic contact, tends to vary with the size of the kinship universe, the number of kin with whom an individual has frequent and intimate contact is usually little different for those with large kinship networks from those with small' (1961, p. 336). And so on reflection there seems to be little point in establishing complete genealogies for people who are never seen and only very rarely interact. My attention has been concentrated on those kin who the families considered important. As mentioned earlier genealogies can be important as a research tool. In several genealogies it was however possible to actually chart the processes of social and geographical mobility from the genealogy itself, e.g. the names of the two eldest children of a cousin (father's brother's) were known, but not the younger

---

4. sex; 5. age; 6. residential distribution of kin; 7. type of housing; 8. occupation; 9. income; 10. leisure activities; 11. religious affiliations; 12. ideas of rights and duties of kinsfolk.

two. It is possible to say that contact was lost somewhere between. In other words in these cases it is possible to infer the process of social mobility from the structure or pattern of social relationships within which it takes place.

The influence of the work of Elizabeth Bott on mine is very great. The importance of her work for mine generally stems from the fact that she also studied ordinary urban families and managed to describe effectively the social environment in which they lived. In particular she related geographical mobility to the type of network of which the family is the centre (1957, p. 107). 'A family's network will become more loose-knit if either the family or other members of the network move away physically or socially' (p. 106). But this book is not really concerned with conjugal relationships and so I infrequently make any direct reference to her work. I ought however to say that although I no longer agree with her on several points, I am attempting to build on many of her insights and findings, paying them (and her) the respect of using them more often than I quote them.

Writers on social mobility have not hesitated to pronounce on the effects of this process on the family and kin. This is familiar ground, so I will not linger long. There seem to be some universal truths that are held to be self-evident as to the effects of social and geographical mobility on the structure of the extended family. David Glass writes that 'actual movement itself may, save in special circumstances (which he does not define) distort or destroy kinship associations, with possible personal and social deprivation' (1954, p. 25). Similarly Schneider and Homans: 'Upward mobile persons keep only shallow ties with members of their kindred, if they keep them at all; downward mobile persons may be neglected by their kindred; members of spatially static groups can but need not' (1955, p. 1204). In the particular middle-class situation in North America, Arensberg and Kimball summarizing wrote, 'the household is small and mobile, enabling the family to follow the husband as he moves from position to position, from one town to another; frequent moves increase the family's isolation not only from kindred but from neighbours and members of a given community' (1965, pp. 232–3). The authors of *Crestwood Heights* argue that even during the earliest stages of the family cycle, 'The newly formed family is frequently isolated geographically and often socially from the parental families' (1956, p. 160). Underlying these randomly selected statements one suspects that there is a crude functionalism, perhaps stated at its baldest by Barber in his textbook. He wrote that there is a 'functional congruence between the isolated nuclear family and individual occupational achievement with its accompanying geographical and social mobility' (1957, p. 364).

It has become part of the folklore of sociology that the extended family hinders geographical mobility. But as Greenfield (1961) pointed out there is no *necessary* causal connection between the nuclear family form of kinship and industrialization. Recently however there has been a tendency to emphasize that even among the most mobile, socially and geographically there may still be some relationship at least between a mother and her married daughter. In his book *The Migratory Elite*, Musgrove wrote that 'the migrant is isolated from his wider kin. This isolation may be welcomed . . though his wife will probably maintain a fairly close contact with her mother even though she is of lower social status, if distances are not too great' (1963, pp. 113–14). Dobriner in describing a somewhat extreme habitat of the geographically mobile American, Levittown, attempted to illustrate the isolation of the elementary family by saying that 'Grandma is only a voice on the phone' (1963, p. 7). But surely the point is that she was a voice on the phone. As I discovered during my fieldwork it is very easy to misinterpret the evidence of family contact amongst the mobile.

Willmott has more realistically written on the evidence of recent studies that 'the kindred may be an important source of companionship in the heart of the modern city' (1958, p. 126). Indeed Firth has gone as far as to suggest that because there is a marked physical separation from the household's kin it increases the possibility of selecting relationships; and that this 'is one of the ways in which urban industrial influences towards individuation and impersonal isolation are counteracted' (1964, p. 85). A particularistic kinship ideology may be of great importance for the individual's emotional needs in an industrial society, though in his behaviour he may be completely committed to a universalistic pattern of relationships. Extended family ties become theoretically possible when universalistic and particularistic value systems are not seen as a continuum pervading all social systems, but as applicable to different systems of society independently of each other.

Possibly the most notable attempt at synthesis between work on the family and that on social and geographical mobility is that of Eugene Litwak (1960 (*a*) (*b*) (*c*) ). His conclusions have direct relevance to my study and can be reduced to five major propositions.

1. That the extended kin family exists in modern urban society, at least among the urban middle class.
2. That extended family relations are possible in an urban industrial society.
3. That geographical propinquity is an unnecessary condition of these relationships.
4. That occupational mobility is unhindered by these activities, such activities as advice, financial assistance, etc. provide aid during such movement.
5. That the classical extended family of rural society or its ethnic counterpart is unsuited to modern society and the isolated nuclear family is not the most functional type. The most functional being what he calls the 'modified extended family'.

He defines the 'modified extended family' as 'a series of nuclear families joined together on an equalitarian basis for mutual aid, not bound by demands for geographic propinquity or occupational similarity' (1960 (*a*), p. 178). Christopher in a research note sums up the evidence on the relationship between industrialization and the family: 'the two are not, as was long thought, inimical to the optimum functioning of each other' (1965, p. 184).

This chapter attempts to continue Litwak's valuable synthesis and to examine in greater detail some functions of the middle class extended family, and in doing so, to analyse the structural supports for these functions. Because if Litwak and others in the United States,[1] and those at the Institute of Community Studies, and Rosser and Harris have qualified the extremer statements about the effects of social and geographical mobility

---

[1] See Axelrod (1956); Greer (1956); Sussman (1955); Sussman and Burchinal (1965); Sussman and Clyde White (1959); Jaco and Balknap (1953).

on the extended family there still remains the belief[1] that the wider kindred are relatively unimportant for the elementary family at least in what Solan Kimball has alliteratively called 'its mobile, metropolitan, middle class manifestation'; when compared with (*a*) the working class or (*b*) those who have been immobile both socially and geographically. Or put the other way those for whom kin are least important are those members of modern industrial society who are middle class and who have been both geographically and socially mobile. The 120 families studied are therefore especially strategic, for testing this hypothesis, having experienced different amounts of geographical and social mobility.

## 2 *Geographical Distribution and Contact*

It will be remembered that the 120 families studied can be divided in the following ways

|  | Socially mobile | Socially immobile |
|---|---|---|
| Geographically mobile | 31 | 69 |
| Geographically immobile | — | 20 |

I am now going to compare the geographical distribution of members of the extended families for the families that I studied with other studies, especially with the two that give details of middle class kin behaviour and distribution: that of Rosser and Harris (1965) and that of Willmott and Young (1960). To anticipate what follows I will show that the families studied have a greater geographical spread, and that contact between them is less than that for middle class samples for Swansea and Woodford. In other words, if I can show that the extended family still has a function under these conditions, and can analyse its structure, I will have been able to further qualify the functionalist view of the family in modern urban society.

Before I launch into details, I must emphasize that in the comparisons that follow I am not comparing like with like. While both Rosser and Harris's and Willmott and Young's studies were based on random samples, mine is not. The figures

[1] See for example Barrie Stacey's recent arguments that 'with mobility family connections become fewer and more tenuous' (B. G. Stacey: 1967, p. 5).

that follow do not suggest that the families I studied have been more geographically mobile and have less contact with their kin than *all* the middle class families in the other two studies, but that they have been more mobile and have less kin contact than is usual for the middle class as a whole in both Swansea and Woodford.[1]

Of the 120 households that form the universe of my study, 109 consisted of elementary families in that they consisted of a husband and his wife, together with their children if any. There were no incomplete elementary families. But in the other eleven households there was one other permanent additional member outside the elementary family. This is in houses that are designed for elementary families and are advertised as such. In no case was there more than one additional member per household. The eleven consisted of one husband's father and one husband's mother, two wives' fathers and five wives' mothers; and two wives' siblings: both sisters. In addition one household had the wife's mother to stay twice a year for two months: she perambulated between her three daughters. So even in these adverse conditions one household in ten had a permanent additional relative outside the elementary family as a member. These eleven 'extra' members of the household are left out of the tables about contact to avoid giving it a purely notional character.

Table 4:1 shows the geographical distribution of close kin: wives' and husbands' parents, siblings, uncles and aunts. I have also produced parts of this table graphically, Diagram (i), and this emphasizes the salient points. It shows that the geographical distribution of different categories of kin is very similar (the vertical axis of the graph representing the proportion of the total number of live kin in a particular category and the horizontal axis represents the distance they are living away by selected points). It shows that there are two main distributions of close kin. Those living in western Swansea and within 25 miles, and those living at and beyond 100 miles. It also shows that there are very few relatives living in eastern Swansea, emphasizing the point that very few of these families have been socially or geographically mobile locally. It also shows that

[1] My technique here and elsewhere is what has been called inter-calibration.

TABLE 4:1  *Geographical distribution of the close kin of 120 middle class families living in Swansea*

| Total | Don't know | Abroad | Dead | | In house-hold | Swansea W. E. | | Within 25 miles | Within 50 miles | Within 100 miles | Plus 100 miles | Total | Total |
|---|---|---|---|---|---|---|---|---|---|---|---|---|---|
| 44 | | 1 | 43 | wife's mother | 5 | 12 | 4 | 19 | 4 | 4 | 28 | 76 | 120 |
| 59 | | 2 | 57 | wife's father | 2 | 9 | 2 | 11 | 5 | 3 | 29 | 61 | 120 |
| 42 | | 3 | 39 | husband's mother | 1 | 17 | 4 | 18 | 4 | 4 | 30 | 78 | 120 |
| 53 | | 3 | 50 | husband's father | 1 | 15 | 3 | 17 | 5 | 3 | 23 | 67 | 120 |
| 41 | | 10 | 31 | wife's siblings | 2 | 34 | 14 | 45 | 14 | 15 | 67 | 191 | 232 |
| 60 | | 20 | 40 | husband's siblings | | 41 | 17 | 40 | 13 | 17 | 62 | 190 | 250 |
| 203 | 15 | 17 | 171 | wife's parents siblings | | 59 | 32 | 71 | 40 | 24 | 174 | 400 | 603 |
| 203 | 8 | 14 | 181 | husband's parents siblings | | 50 | 24 | 74 | 44 | 34 | 153 | 379 | 582 |
| 705 | 23 | 70 | 612 | Totals | 11 | 237 | 100 | 295 | 129 | 104 | 566 | 1441 | 2147 |
| 2 | | 2 | | Children | 158 | 5 | | 1 | | | 4 | 168 | 170 |
| 32.9 | 1.1 | 3.3 | 28.5% (excluding children) | | 0.5 | 11.1 | 4.7 | 13.7 | 6.0 | 4.8 | 26.3 | 67.1 | 100% |

DIAGRAM (i):

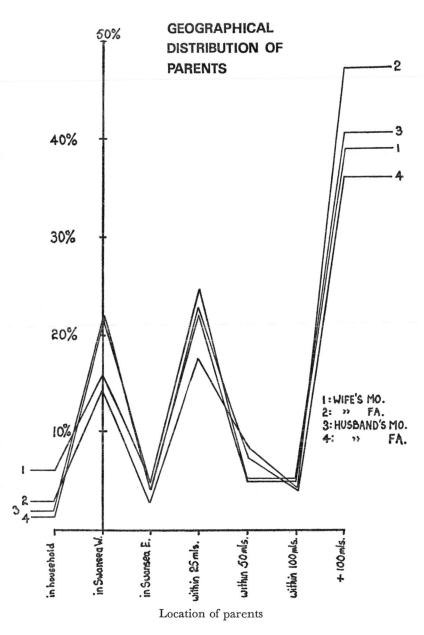

**GEOGRAPHICAL DISTRIBUTION OF PARENTS**

1: WIFE'S MO.
2: " FA.
3: HUSBAND'S MO.
4: " FA.

Location of parents

there is no difference in the geographical distribution of husbands' parents when compared with wives' parents. (This basic distribution of close kin is very important to the major conclusions of this research because it shows that there were two types of middle class families: those with the core of their kin-group living within 25 miles and those with them living beyond 100 miles.)

TABLE 4:2 *Proximity of married subjects to parents: comparing with Rosser and Harris's sample (see Tables 6:1 and 6:2)*

| Parents' residence | Rosser and Harris: 791 married people with at least one parent alive | | | | | | 170 with at least 1 parent alive. The two estates | |
|---|---|---|---|---|---|---|---|---|
| | Working classes | | Middle classes | | Total | | | |
| | Marr. Sons | Marr. Daus. | Marr. Sons | Marr. Daus. | Marr. Sons | Marr. Daus. | Marr. Sons | Marr. Daus. |
| | % | % | % | % | % | % | % | % |
| Same locality in Swansea | 24 | 46 | 34 | 30 | 26 | 42 | 23 | 14 |
| Other locality in Swansea | 51 | 39 | 26 | 33 | 45 | 38 | 5 | 5 |
| Region around up to 12 miles | 8 | 5 | 12 | 5 | 9 | 5 | 16 | 14 |
| Elsewhere | 17 | 10 | 28 | 32 | 20 | 15 | 56 | 67 |
| Total % | 100 | 100 | 100 | 100 | 100 | 100 | 100 | 100 |
| Number | 289 | 311 | 94 | 97 | 383 | 408 | 85 | 85 |

Table 4:2 shows the proximity or otherwise of married subjects to parents as compared with Rosser and Harris's sample, distinguishing between married sons and daughters. Rosser and Harris found that only 20% of all married sons and 15% of all married daughters with at least one parent alive, were living more than 12 miles from this parent. By social class these figures dropped to 17% and 10% for the working class

and rose to 28% and 32% for the middle class. The figures for my families are 56% and 67% for sons and daughters respectively: this is almost double the number that Rosser and Harris had for the middle class members of their sample. Both my figures and Rosser and Harris's show a tendency for middle class sons to be living closer to their parents than are their wives. This is not as marked as the opposite tendency among the working class: that of wives living closer to their parents than their husbands' parents, but it is nevertheless noticeable. 23% of the men in the families I studied lived in the same locality as their parents as opposed to 14% of the women. And as mentioned above, 67% of married daughters' parents live beyond 12 miles as opposed to 56% of married sons'. However, as Diagram (i) shows, these differences are obscured if 'same locality' is broadened to western Swansea and the twelve-mile cut-off point extended to 25 miles.

TABLE 4:3   *Parents' residence according to social class of informant*

| Parents' residence | Woodford* | | Bethnal Green* | Swansea† | | The two estates |
|---|---|---|---|---|---|---|
| | Middle class | Working class | | Middle class | Working class | |
| | % | % | % | % | % | % |
| Same locality | 14 | 21 | 31 | 32 | 35 | 18·5 |
| Elsewhere in borough | 12 | 21 | 13 | 29·5 | 45 | 5·0 |
| Outside borough | 74 | 58 | 46 | 38·5 | 20 | 76·5 |
| Total % | 100 | 100 | 100 | 100 | 100 | 100 |
| Number | 242 | 152 | 369 | 191 | 600 | 170 |

* Willmott & Young (1960), Table XI, p. 78 (combined 'same dwelling' and 'Within 5 minutes' walk' same locality).

† Rosser and Harris (1965), Table 6:2, p. 213 (combined columns 1 and 2; 3 and 4. And 'Region Around' plus 'Elsewhere' = Outside Borough).

Table 4:3 carries the comparison of the geographical distribution of parental residence to Bethnal Green and to Woodford. The most striking thing about this table is the similarity between my figures and those for the middle class in Willmott and Young's Woodford sample. 74% of the Woodford middle class parents lived outside the borough and 76·9% of mine lived outside Swansea. This is to be compared with 38·5% of Rosser and Harris's which is lower even than the figure for Bethnal Green.

I should also point out that Tables 4:1, 2 and 3 show that only 5% of the families I studied have parents in other localities in Swansea, even less if this is limited to eastern Swansea. (Compared with 29·5% of Rosser and Harris's middle class sample.) This again emphasizes that they have experienced remarkably little geographical mobility within the borough. That is to say that those families who have been geographically, and as it turned out socially mobile have come from beyond the Borough boundaries rather than from elsewhere in Swansea. And about a quarter were brought up in the same locality of Swansea as they are now living, i.e. high status middle class areas, and have been therefore neither socially

TABLE 4:4    *Area of upbringing compared with Rosser and Harris: Table 2:2*

| Area brought up | Rosser and Harris main sample | | | The two estates | | | | | |
|---|---|---|---|---|---|---|---|---|---|
| | | | | Husbands | | | Wives | | |
| | Numbers | % | % | Numbers | % | % | Numbers | % | % |
| Locality of Swansea in which now living | 663 | 33⎫ | | 20 | 17⎫ | | 17 | 14⎫ | |
| Other locality within Swansea | 807 | 41⎭ | 74 | 9 | 7⎭ | 24 | 8 | 7⎭ | 21 |
| Region around up to 12 miles | 116 | 6⎫ | | 11 | 9⎫ | | 8 | 7⎫ | |
| Elsewhere in Wales | 130 | 7⎬ | 26 | 24 | 19⎬ | 76 | 24 | 19⎬ | 79 |
| Elsewhere | 246 | 13⎭ | | 56 | 48⎭ | | 63 | 53⎭ | |
| Total | 1962 | 100 | 100 | 120 | 100 | 100 | 120 | 100 | 100 |

nor geographically mobile. Again this is important to my overall analysis: there are two groups: those who have been geographically mobile and those who have not.

Table 4:4 emphasizes these points: both the geographical mobility of most of the families I studied compared with the experience of most of the middle class of Swansea; and the dichotomy between the mobile and non-mobile families. This table shows the area of upbringing of the families I studied compared with Rosser and Harris. 74% of their sample were brought up in Swansea and 26% outside, of whom 20% were brought up further than 12 miles from Swansea. On the other hand in the families I studied 24% of the husbands were brought up in Swansea and 21% of the wives. 76% of the husbands and 79% of the wives were brought up outside the borough, of which 67% and 72% respectively were brought up further than 12 miles from Swansea.

A general picture emerges of most of the families living at some distance from their parents and having been brought up away from Swansea; and of a smaller group who have always lived in the borough, probably always in the more select parts of western Swansea and whose parents are living in the same locality.

Against this background of the geographical distribution of members of the extended family, I would like now to turn to contact between members. But first I would like to make some reservations about 'contact' as a measure of anything, especially the structure and function of the extended family. It is very difficult to know exactly what 'contact' means and as I said earlier it is easy to misinterpret the evidence of family contact amongst the mobile. This must be emphasized especially when definitions of the extended family such as that of Peter Townsend depend on 'daily or almost daily contact' (1964, p. 92). In the case of the families I studied if this definition was adopted there would be very few kin groupings that would qualify. It is necessary to look in depth at these relations and not to place too much reliance on this apparently precise measure of the extended family. One can however hypothesize an inverse relationship between distance and frequency of contact between kin.

The technique will continue to be to compare my findings

with other studies. Table 4:5 shows frequency of contact with parent.

TABLE 4:5 *Frequency of contact with parents (married persons only with parent concerned alive)—percentages*

| Last seen | Rosser and Harris Table 6:3 | | | | The two estates | | | |
|---|---|---|---|---|---|---|---|---|
| | Mothers | | Fathers | | Mothers | | Fathers | |
| | *Marr. sons* | *Marr. daus.* | *Marr. sons* | *Marr. daus.* | *Marr. sons* | *Marr. daus.* | *Marr. sons* | *Marr. daus.* |
| Within last 24 hours | 31 | 54 | 29 | 47 | 12 | 13 | 10 | 5 |
| Within last week | 40 | 27 | 41 | 30 | 24 | 29 | 18 | 27 |
| Week–month ago | 14 | 7 | 15 | 9 | 27 | 24 | 28 | 32 |
| Less frequently | 15 | 12 | 15 | 14 | 37 | 34 | 44 | 36 |
| Total % | 100 | 100 | 100 | 100 | 100 | 100 | 100 | 100 |
| Number | 345 | 348 | 237 | 254 | 78 | 77 | 70 | 63 |

Perhaps the most important figure is that whilst in Rosser and Harris's sample 54% of married daughters had seen their mother in the last 24 hours only 13% of the wives I studied had. 19% of married daughters in Rosser and Harris's sample had *not* seen their mothers in the last week whereas 58% of mine had not. Table 4:6 emphasizes this contrast. The really relevant comparison here is with Rosser and Harris's figures for the middle class. In their sample 74% of the sons and 76% of the daughters had seen their mothers in the last week whereas the figures for my families are 36% and 42% respectively. The striking thing about Rosser and Harris's table is the similarity between the middle class and the working class contact rates, although the middle class figures tend to be slightly lower. But the contact rates between my families and their parents is in most cases less than half that of Rosser and Harris.

Tables 4:7 and 8 show the difference in contact rates between

TABLE 4:6  *Frequency of contact with parents, by social class of subject—(percentages)*

| | Rosser and Harris: Table 6:4 | | | | | | | | The two estates | | | |
| | Mothers | | | | Fathers | | | | Mothers | | Fathers | |
| | Middle classes | | Working classes | | Middle classes | | Working classes | | | | | |
| | Sons | Daus. | Sons | Daus. | Sons | Daus. | Sons | Daus. | Sons | Daus. | Sons | Daus. |
|---|---|---|---|---|---|---|---|---|---|---|---|---|
| Within 24 hours | 39 | 44 | 27 | 56 | 37 | 39 | 26 | 48 | 12 | 13 | 10 | 5 |
| 24 hours–1 week | 35 | 32 | 43 | 27 | 26 | 28 | 45 | 31 | 24 | 29 | 18 | 27 |
| Total % within 1 week | 74 | 76 | 70 | 83 | 63 | 67 | 71 | 79 | 36 | 42 | 28 | 32 |
| Numbers | 97 | 91 | 248 | 256 | 57 | 64 | 180 | 190 | 78 | 77 | 70 | 63 |

mother and married daughter in Swansea, Bethnal Green, Woodford and amongst the families I studied.

TABLE 4:7  *Contact with mothers: married daughters with mothers alive*

|  | Bethnal Green | Woodford | Swansea* | The two estates |
|---|---|---|---|---|
|  | % | % | % | % |
| Seen within previous 24 hours | 43 | 30 | 42·5 | 12 |
| Seen earlier in previous week | 31 | 33 | 33·5 | 27 |
| Not seen within previous week | 26 | 37 | 24·0 | 61 |
| Total % | 100 | 100 | 100 | 100 |
| Number | 290 | 246 | 693 | 155 |

* Combined columns 1 and 2, Table 6:3, Rosser and Harris, p. 219.

TABLE 4:8  *Contact with mothers and fathers: daughters with mother/father alive*

|  | Woodford* | | Swansea† | | The two estates | |
|---|---|---|---|---|---|---|
|  | Mothers | Fathers | Mothers | Fathers | Mothers | Fathers |
| Seen in previous 24 hours | 30 | 25 | 42·5 | 38 | 12 | 7 |
| Seen earlier in previous week | 33 | 34 | 33·5 | 35·5 | 27 | 21 |
| Not seen in previous week | 37 | 41 | 24·0 | 16·5 | 61 | 72 |
| Total % | 100 | 100 | 100 | 100 | 100 | 100 |
| Number | 346 | 234 | 693 | 491 | 155 | 133 |

* Woodford: Table VIII, p. 66.
† Swansea: from Table 6:3, p. 219.

The overall similarity between Swansea and Bethnal Green is brought out, whilst the figures that come closest to mine are those for Woodford. But even there 30% of married daughters had seen their mothers in the previous 24 hours compared with 12% of mine, and only 37% had not seen their mothers in the last week compared with 61% of mine.

Contact with fathers shows a very similar overall pattern in different localities to that with mothers, but the amount of contact being somewhat less.

Table 4:9 shows contact with siblings. Information was collected about 231 wives' siblings and 250 husbands' siblings.

TABLE 4:9   *Contact with siblings*

|  | Wife | | Husband | |
|---|---|---|---|---|
|  | *Number* | % | *Number* | % |
| Within last 24 hours | 13 | 5·8 | 18 | 7·2 |
| last week | 39 | 16·8 | 55 | 22·0 |
| last month | 61 | 26·0 | 55 | 22·0 |
| last year | 82 | 34·8 | 81 | 32·4 |
| Longer than year | 22 | 9·7 | 15 | 6·0 |
| Abroad | 3 | 1·4 | 10 | 4·0 |
| Dead | 3 | 1·4 | 8 | 3·2 |
| Do NOT see | 6 | 2·9 | 8 | 3·2 |
| Lives with | 2 | ·8 | — | — |
| Total % | 231 | 100 | 250 | 100 |

20 wives with no siblings.
21 husbands with no siblings.

Rosser and Harris say of sibling contact that 'just over half the men we interviewed and two-thirds of the women had seen a brother or a sister living apart in the last week' (1965, p. 222), whereas less than one-third of the men and just over one-fifth of the women of the families that I studied had seen a sibling in the last week. And though they say that the frequencies are slightly lower for the middle classes, mine are much lower than their overall totals for Swansea.

An indication of the inadequacy of direct frequency of contact as a measure and indicator of the structure and function of the extended family can be shown for example by the use of the telephone. Just over a quarter (33) had telephoned a wife's parent in the last week and a fifth (22) had rung a husband's parent in the same period. A similar proportion had rung siblings (19). Similarly 48 households had written to the wife's parents in the last month and 46 to the husband's parents. With the increasing frequency of car ownership, sheer physical distance becomes less of an obstacle to contact between relatives. All but four of the households on these two estates had at least one car and all but nine had a telephone.

In conclusion to this section the basic characteristics of the extended families of the 120 households I studied can be said to be a wide geographical dispersion together with a lack of day-to-day contact when compared with the population of Swansea as a whole or even with the middle class within that sample. Yet in these seemingly adverse conditions I hope to be able to show that the extended family is a functioning institution even amongst the most mobile. But unless the families are studied in some depth, it would be possible to argue from much of the evidence assembled above that these are isolated elementary families. I hope to show that actual geographical distance seems unimportant. Families are free to live where they choose and their relationship with their kin does not depend on frequency of contact. Geographical mobility may affect the type of interaction pattern (e.g. rates of contact as discussed above) but there seems to be no reason why it should result in a lessening of ideological and emotional commitment to kin and/or disrupt relations between kin altogether.

Despite, and in some cases because of, the distance between members of the middle class extended family, it does have functional importance. By analysing some aspects of its function I hope to be able to show that there are some aspects of its structure that should be emphasized which have hitherto been somewhat overshadowed by the past emphasis on the mother/married-daughter link.

It is interesting to compare the 120 middle class families I studied with the results of the L.S.E. Highgate study from their published material (Firth: 1964, Crozier: 1965, Hubert: 1965). The major difference between the two studies is that among the L.S.E. families there were no 'locals'—this is a reflection of the metropolitan nature of their sample. And Hubert found that 'contact' rates were inflated by their sample being in London and suggests that they would be lower in a more provincial town (1965, p. 76). A comparison of my Tables 4:1 to 4:9 with her Tables I and II (pp. 71, 72) would appear to confirm this. Crozier can say of English middle class society in the eighteenth and nineteenth centuries that it has two important characteristics: 'the social and geographical mobility of its members and the range of economic opportunity open to them' (1965, p. 15), of the families she studied in Highgate she can say that their 'kin universe extended throughout England and further afield' (p. 8). An analysis of the birthplace of 145 heads of households in the 1851 Census gives the following (pp. 17—18):

TABLE 4:10

|  |  |  |
|---|---|---|
|  | 6 males | Highgate |
|  | 1 female |  |
|  | 53 males | in other metropolitan |
|  | 12 females | parishes |
|  | 62 males | elsewhere in the U.K. |
|  | 10 females | or abroad |
| Total | 145 |  |

In fact these figures are closer to my families than those of any contemporary study; and Crozier shows that even with this geographical mobility and consequent wide distribution of kin there was an extended family functioning at this time. It is not irrelevant for one of the major conclusions of this research that in her summary she says that 'It would appear however that while the maternal kin played an important role in the life of any individual as they do in most societies, the important structural principle was patrimonial' (p. 40). However in mid-nineteenth century Highgate there seemed to be very few locals.

## 3  Structure and Function

During the fieldwork I became aware of apparent conflicts between various remarks about the role of the family made by my informants. Conflicting statements were made even by the same informants at different times. This was evidence of an ambiguous attitude towards the extended family which was emphasized by the conflict between the overall stress on independence and the evidence that I collected that they were the recipients of considerable and continuing extended family aid.

I became interested in how the families I was studying resolved the contradiction between the ubiquitous 'blood is thicker than water' and 'you can't keep going to see your parents'. Between being told that one ought to 'turn to the family first' and 'one has to stand on one's own'. And between being told that 'all the family should stick together' and that 'you have to make your own way'. It was in attempting to isolate the mechanisms by which the elementary family receives aid from the extended family whilst maintaining an appearance of independence that I discovered it was necessary to reanalyse a great deal of my field material, which led me to emphasize certain aspects of the middle class extended family's structure. These apparent contradictions are in fact a statement of the alternatives that faced the families I studied. They must not be seen as mutually exclusive but as a realization of the room for manœuvre within the system (see Clyde Mitchell's introduction to Van Velsen (1964)).

On the basis of the American evidence it has been argued that the middle class extended family is used as 'a principal source of aid and service when member families are in personal difficulties or in times of disaster and crisis and on ceremonial occasions' (Sussman and Burchinal: 1962, p. 234). Although I collected data about crisis situations and ceremonial occasions I do not want to present it here. I aimed to describe ordinary families and I want to emphasize the ordinary rather than the unusual. It is central to my argument that middle class extended family aid is not dependent upon crisis and ceremonial; and that it is not only on these occasions that the middle class extended family is a functioning social entity but that it works continually, if not day to day then month to month, to maintain and/or advance the status of its members.

Mutual aid between members of an extended family flows in several directions depending upon stages in the family cycle. Most of the families that I have been studying are in the first two stages of the family cycle:[1] that of 'home-making' and 'child-rearing'. These two stages are the time of greatest expenditure and, because of the nature of the middle class career pattern, the time of lowest income (see section on the nature of middle class career patterns). Whereas the large literature of gerontology (see Townsend: 1964) has added to our knowledge of the structure and function of the family, through the study of support and aid flowing towards the final stage of the family cycle, I know of no systematic study of support and aid flowing towards the first two stages of the family cycle.

The basic demography of the 120 families is shown in Diagram (ii) which is an age 'pyramid' for the husbands and wives. It shows that 55% of the husbands are in their 30's and only 24% are over 45. By stage in the family cycle, the families are as follows:

TABLE 4:11   *Stage in family life cycle*

|              | No. | %  |
|--------------|-----|----|
| Home making  | 31  | 26 |
| Child rearing| 80  | 67 |
| Dispersal    | 7   | 6  |
| Final        | 2   | 1  |

These figures demonstrate that most of these families are passing through the stages in the family cycle of greatest need.

The kind of aid that I am discussing is not exceptional aid in exceptional times. Shaw, writing about a predominantly working class London suburb, gives a very fine example of what I mean. One of the very few professional families she studied reported that the husband's mother and father had bought a new winter outfit for the first child when the expense of the second left them short of money (1954, p. 185). This is an example of the middle class extended family providing important and significant increments of aid for the idiosyncratic needs of the elementary family. There was no need for geographical proximity.

---

[1] Definitions of stages in the family cycle.
   1. Home making: from marriage to the birth of first child.
   2. Child rearing: from birth of first child until marriage of first child.
   3. Dispersal: from marriage of first child until marriage of last child.
   4. Final: from marriage of last child until death of original partners.

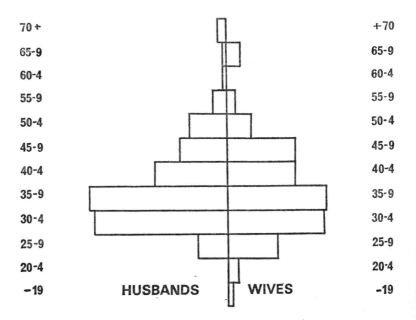

**DIAGRAM (ii) : AGE PYRAMID**

The ability, although not the desire, to provide this type of aid will vary with social class. As Fletcher has written:

'the kinds and degrees of mutual aid and the reasons for it, may differ between social classes. For example, young middle class parents may desire, and obtain, help from older relatives in order to send their children to public schools; or they may want their *father's* (my emphasis) influence in prevailing upon a friendly solicitor so that they can purchase their house with minimum legal costs and beyond such financial aid and influence there may be little sentimental attachment and little desire for closer inter-dependence. Young working class parents on the other hand will not and cannot expect or require these degrees of financial aid of their elder relatives and their problems will be different and they may express deeper sentimental feelings of attach-ment' (1962, p. 170).

This last point I feel can be doubted. Middle class kin networks may have fewer day-to-day demands but I think that there is little evidence to suggest that they necessarily show any different affective quality. The results of this research would lead me to disagree with Townsend when he writes that 'although much close investigation of middle class family life, particularly in outlying districts of Britain's cities remains to be done, the evidence that has so far emerged suggests only small variations in function and frequency of contact from working class life (1963, pp. 240–1). I hope that I have shown that measures of contact are very dubious for families that are geographically scattered and also I hope to show that the middle class extended family performs functions that the working class extended family cannot, through financial inability rather than differences in sentiment. Perhaps it would be most sensible to follow Fletcher's conclusions 'The truth is quite simply that more research is needed here before we can know reliably what regional and social differences there are' (1962, p. 170).

Before I go into a more detailed discussion of some of my field material may I suggest that all the data I have gathered are likely to be underestimations. These topics are considered private and most of it was gleaned indirectly. Most of the remainder of this section is therefore qualitative rather than quantitative.

It became apparent that in certain spheres of social activity aid from kin was more important than in others. So I pursued these topics, together with collecting more general kin information. The topics I concentrated on were careers, housing and their children. In examining these subjects—which in many cases are the dominant interests of the families I studied—I found that over and over again where there had been aid from the extended family the important structural link between members of the extended family was the father-in-law/father-son/son-in-law link. This led me to reanalyse a great deal of my field material.

In doing so I felt very similar to Aberle and Naegele who in a paper on the socialization of middle class children in the United States wrote that 'One reason we are stressing the father is that he is forgotten or recedes into the background in the face of the overwhelming focus on the mother in recent work' (1952, p. 367). Or in my case the overwhelming focus on the mother–married daughter link in recent work. The father–

son link is structurally important in the middle class extended family because through it flows aid to the elementary family.

Here I would like to take an 'apt illustration' from my field notes. (The speaker is a 37-year-old geographically mobile but socially immobile architect, m.q. = 44·4.)

'I wanted to leave the firm I was working for and buy into a practice as a partner. I had had a very attractive offer. But I wanted a couple of hundred more than I had. When we went home (to a town in the Midlands which both husband and wife came from and returned to visit parents about four times a year) I went to the local with my father-in-law (his father is dead) and told him I was considering changing my job like I said. I didn't ask but to tell the truth I hoped. He said "How much?" and I told him and he said that he would see. Eventually he gave it to me, called it a loan but said I needn't pay it back. But I am though—£5 a month so I don't feel obligated to him. I didn't ask my bank because they were also the firm's bank and you know Rotary and that. It was easier to ask him.'

He told me that he would have approached his father had he been alive. As Rosser and Harris have pointed out in their paper on relationships through marriage one function of affinal relationships under certain circumstances is for them to be utilized as substitutes for missing consanguineal kin (1961, p. 318). This is well documented by Young and Willmott, and Townsend for the working class mother–daughter link. It would seem that substitution (in the sense of role adoption) can also be found in the middle class father–son link. In a bilateral system such as ours there is always the possibility of alternatives within the structure.

This illustration also shows that the recipient felt less obligation for accepting aid since he did not ask for it; also it illustrates a recurrent mechanism. The money was not asked for, the case was stated and the action was left up to the parent. In this way there seems to be at least a partial resolve of the conflict between the stress on independence and actual dependence. Physical distance allows the recipients to maintain an appearance of independence and the ubiquity of financial institutions means that distance is irrelevant to aid of this kind. Jane Hubert wrote: 'It is not the "done thing" to be on the receiving end of kin help and influence, but to use one's influence is quite acceptable. Though they do not necessarily see it in these terms, status is conferred by giving not receiving' (1965, p. 68). Diagram (ii) and the table on p. 89 show that as the majority of the 120 families studied are in the first two stages of the family cycle and at the beginning of a middle class career, they are disproportionately on the receiving end of extended family aid.

In contrast to the first example let me quote an example of a 35-year-old geographically mobile but socially immobile insurance man (m.q. = 46·3).

'My father was hurt I think when he knew I went to the bank rather than him for a down payment on a new car but if I'd gone to him for it, the money I mean, we would have had to go there for our holidays. We did anyway, but we didn't have to.'

By going to an institution rather than his father he thought he avoided obligations and kept his independence.

In another case I found that the need could be stated to siblings, but the parents were not told directly. The siblings however were quite expected to tell their parents who were expected to act on this information.

Another mechanism was secrecy or quasi-secrecy. (Speaking is a 34-year-old geographically mobile but socially immobile engineer, m.q. = 46·9.)

'When we had the last baby my father said we should have a home help regularly—very practical man, my dad. He said he would leave the knitting to mum and my sisters but he would pay for the woman and he said not to tell mum as she thought we should be independent. I told Jane (his wife) of course.'

The 'independence' here clearly refers to monetary independence. This case-study is also interesting in that it illustrates the invasion of the sphere usually dominated by the mother–daughter relationship by that of the father and son.

Another mechanism frequently utilized by the families I studied is the giving of aid on socially approved occasions: this is acceptable and can be received without any loss of independence. This begins at the wedding: I recorded one case of the house being given outright and two cases of a substantial deposit being put down on the house. In these cases naturally arrangements were made through the bank but it was the father or father-in-law that made them. This mechanism continues at Christmas and at birthdays—I noted a case of central heating being given as a Christmas present from the husband's parents.

Indirect aid may be given through the children, i.e. from grandparents to grandchildren. When as in one case a lump sum of £100 was given to 'buy things for the baby' it was grandfather who signed the cheque.

This is of course an indirect way of raising the standard of living of the recipients, because it releases money to be spent on other things. In the words of one informant extended family aid 'makes things that much easier'. Extended family aid often is used to provide important status props and helps in the purchase of status signs. I have already mentioned central heating: an important indicator of status amongst the families that I studied, as was having regular help in the home. Another case from my field notes: speaking is the wife of a geographically mobile but socially immobile chemist (m.q. = 42·9).

> 'Dad gave me £20 to buy Jim (her 14-year-old son) a bike for his birthday—he knew that we were going to buy him one anyway. So we got a new carpet as well (and then very quickly and somewhat guiltily.) Aren't I awful! But without little bits like that I don't know how we would live here.'

The giving of status props to children: the expensive 'toys' like the bicycle mentioned above or a trampoline was not uncommon. Whilst I was doing the fieldwork great pressure was being put on several parents by their young daughters to be allowed to have riding lessons. This expensive and status conferring pastime was initiated by one girl whose grandfather was paying for them. Another example I have is the paying for ballet lessons by an uncle (husband's father's brother).

It is not coincidence that all my examples are taken from informants who have not been socially mobile, i.e. have middle class parents. Working class parents would very rarely be in a position to give aid of the proportions described above. If no geographical mobility had been experienced mothers could still give aid to their daughters of the kind described by Willmott and Young and others for the working class. But none of the families studied had been socially mobile *and* geographically immobile. Consequently there seems to have been a readjustment in emphasis in the structure of the extended family away from the mother–daughter relationship towards the father–son relationship.

The exact effects of extended family aid flowing between father and son is very difficult to determine especially as it was impossible to collect this information systematically and uniformly. But as a rough guide I compared the ages of husbands who had been socially mobile, i.e. had come from manual homes with those who had come from middle class backgrounds. The hypothesis being that the estates could be seen as a certain status level and that those who were in the theoretical position to receive extended family aid would reach this status level sooner than those who were not in a position to receive extended family aid. For example this was very noticeable in the case of a 25-year-old bank clerk, who could only have been classified as 'junior non-manual' living on the estate who was the recipient of a great deal of financial assistance from both his father and father-in-law. It turned out that the 31 socially mobile husbands were on average 2·1 years older than those from middle class backgrounds. It would not be correct to put this 2·1 years advantage down completely to extended family aid but as a socially mobile informant told me 'there's a lot of what I call real money here, you know family money, we lived in a two-roomed flat when we started, but look at them'. She was referring to a family who had moved to the estate on marriage.

The variable of social mobility was far more important to the function of the middle class extended family than was geographical mobility. Osterreich (1965) compared 45 English speaking middle class Canadians who were homogeneous in all other respects and compared those who had been geographically mobile with those who had not. She found that the greatest difference between the mobile and the non-mobile was in caring for children, help during illness, taking care of the house and advice on personal matters. In other words the greatest differences were in those actions that depended on availability at short notice and/or physical presence. She found that she could support Litwak's hypothesis (see introduction to this Chapter). But she quite ignores the factor of social mobility which seriously detracts from her findings. The amount of aid is likely to be very different for those from middle class backgrounds when compared with those from working class backgrounds.

95

(Before stating the major conclusions to this chapter I would like in parentheses to compare the role of the organization that employs the husband with the extended family because there are some startling similarities. The organization can also provide status props, the source of which may also be concealed from the neighbours, e.g. a second car or the house itself. There is similar reluctance to become 'obligated' to the organization, e.g. by participating in its favourable house purchase scheme or its non-contributable but equally non-transferable pension scheme. Colleagues also act as 'bridges to the wider community' in Young and Willmott's phrase describing relatives in Bethnal Green, putting up new arrivals while they are looking for houses, introducing them around, taking the husbands Sunday drinking and the wives shopping.)

## 4   Conclusions

The conclusions of this chapter have relevance in three areas of sociological research, two of which I have been specifically discussing here: those of the family and social mobility. The third conclusion concerned social relationships on the actual estates, which for the sake of completeness I will mention here but will be elaborated in greater detail in a later chapter of the book.

John Mogey has said that 'mobility creates neighbours in the place of kindred' (quoted in Klein: 1965, p. 131); while this may be true in terms of day-to-day contact this is not true in terms of their long-term importance. The gregariousness of the estates can in part be explained because the day-to-day needs of the families (fulfilled by kin in working-class areas such as Bethnal Green and Morriston) are for the geographically mobile fulfilled by the neighbours. Because, to use a favourite cliché of my informants, they are 'all in the same boat', i.e. in the child rearing stage of the family cycle and in the relatively early stages of a middle class career, they cannot, even if they wanted to, provide the sort of aid I have described above. They can and do, however, co-operate together in building garages, drives, patios and in landscaping gardens, to cut costs. Only superficially have neighbours replaced kindred, for the mobile middle class at least.

Secondly, there are conclusions about the structure of the

middle class extended family. The analysis of aid amongst members of the extended family has emphasized the structural importance of the relationship between father-in-law/father-son/son-in-law. Consequently I would like to qualify both Willmott and Young's (1960, pp. 126–7) and Rosser and Harris's (1965, p. 289) statements to the effect that 'the key relationship within the extended family is that consisting of wife's mother-wife-husband-husband's mother'. Amongst the middle class who have been geographically mobile, where frequent contact between mother and daughter is not possible, there is a need to lay greater stress on the male part of the structure.[1] In the middle class context many wives have been independent before marriage. 31 of the wives in this study had lived away from home for at least two years before marriage and so it is unlikely that they will be very dependent on their mothers, at least for day-to-day emotional needs. I hope however that I do not give the impression that I underestimate the importance of the mother–daughter link but I hope to put right a certain imbalance in the discussion of the structure of the extended family, at least for the middle class. Perhaps it is best to re-emphasize that in a bilateral system there is a choice between the two sides. Empirical research has shown that in the working class context there is a bias towards the mother–married daughter link and I hope I have shown that in the middle class context there is a bias towards the father–son link. Neither bias which emerges from the empirical research should be allowed to mask the symmetrical nature of the structure of the extended family, at least in theory.

Thirdly and finally on what is my prime concern: social mobility. I would like to quote Lipset and Bendix who from behind great ramparts of documentation conclude that 'Many middle class fathers in salaried positions have little to give their children except a good education and motivation to obtain a high status position' (1959, p. 59). This ideology runs throughout most studies of social mobility. I hope I have shown that this is not so and that aid from the extended family can whet the cutting edge of social advancement. Extended family aid in the

---

[1] This may not just apply to the geographically mobile members of the middle class. See for example Stacey (1960), p. 125 on the 'Makepiece' family.

middle class context has to do with standard of living and only very rarely with occupational appointments. Extended family aid does not really operate in the occupational dimension and this is often the only dimension of social mobility that is studied. The standard works on social mobility, by their concentration on the occupation/status dimension to the exclusion of all others, e.g. property, where extended family aid is more important, have missed important variables. When Parsons in *The Social System* maintains that an equal start is impossible in a society in which an 'occupationally differentiated industrial system and a significantly solitary kinship system' (1951, p. 161) are combined, he is correct if it is remembered that for most of the middle class at least, kin aid is towards their standard of living and has little or nothing to do with the occupational system as such.[1]

In fact what I am saying, and this should not come as a surprise to anyone, is that descent is still important and the fundamental unit of the class structure is the family. Both deserve a greater place in the study of social mobility than has hitherto been accorded to them. Herein lies the difficulty. For as G. D. H. Cole wrote in his paper, 'The conception of the Middle Classes', 'In modern fluid societies, the family ceases in more and more instances to be a unit assignable to a single class. This does not mean that classes lose reality but it does mean that their boundaries become more and more difficult to draw' (1950, p. 94). This echoes Schumpeter who wrote that 'the family not the physical person is the true unit of class and class theory' (1950, p. 148). This must be taken into account in an analysis of social mobility. There are some underemphasized aspects of the structure of the middle class extended family that allow it to perform functions relevant to the study of social mobility: in particular the male link that is the means by which the elder middle class generation channels financial aid to the next generation.

[1] S. Thernstrom (in 1964) has shown in his historical study of 'Yankee City' that the concentration of the occupational/status dimension of social mobility totally obscures the property mobility that was taking place. Manual workers begat manual workers but meanwhile they bought houses.

CHAPTER FIVE

# Ceremonial

## 1 *Introduction*

In Chapter Four the data that were collected systematically and uniformly for all 120 households living on the two estates regarding the geographical distribution of and contact between members of the extended family was presented. As already emphasized, it is necessary to go beyond these data and so the material about aid which was not collected systematically was used as 'apt illustration' as a basis for discussion. In this part of the book three genealogies will be analysed in some detail, both in relation to social and geographical mobility and also to compare three christenings. Each christening will represent three major subdivisions into which the 120 families have been divided.

They have been given fictitious names: Murrow, for the socially *and* geographically mobile family; Jackson, for the socially immobile *but* geographically mobile family; and Evans for the socially *and* geographically immobile family. Although complete genealogies for 32 families were collected, they are only used in the tables below to allow the three that are presented to be placed in context and to give some indication of their representativeness or otherwise.

The basic facts about the 32 genealogies that were collected are as follows: the 32 households were made up of:

TABLE 5:1

|  | Socially mobile | Socially immobile |
|---|---|---|
| Geographically mobile | 9 (31) | 17 (69) |
| Geographically immobile | — | 6 (20) |

(The figures in brackets represent the totals for the 120 families studied.) By the number of kin they recognized they can be divided as follows (including dead kin).

TABLE 5:2

*Number of kin recognized*

| | |
|---|---|
| Between 100 and 202* | 16 |
| Between 50 and 99 | 10⎫ |
| Less than 50 | 6⎭ |
| | 32 |

\* One household = 202.

The average number of recognized kin by each of the three major categories was as follows:

TABLE 5:3

| | |
|---|---|
| Socially *and* geographically mobile | 43 |
| Socially immobile *but* geographically mobile | 79 |
| Socially *and* geographically immobile | 142 |

The percentage of dead kin included in each genealogy varied from 8% to 34% and did not vary significantly with social or geographical mobility—in fact it was most closely related to age, as would be expected.

The three families that are being used as 'apt illustration' rather than ideal types can be related to these overall figures (see Table 5:4). It will be seen that they are not atypical except that the local family was a good deal larger. These three were chosen because they all had christenings during the fieldwork and I have to use the Evans family because they were the only local family with whom I developed sufficient 'rapport' to collect detailed information that had a christening during the fieldwork. The exotic nature of the Evans kinship universe serves its purpose if only to throw into contrast the Murrow and Jackson christenings. As Clyde Mitchell has strongly written of case material, 'the typicality of the material is irrelevant since the regularities are set out in the description of the overall social structure'. (Which I hope I have at least gone some way towards doing in the previous chapters.) He continues 'in a sense the more atypical the actions and events described in the case history, the more instructive they are, since the anthropologist uses case material to show how variations can be contained within the structure' (1964, p. xiii).

TABLE 5:4  Summary of characteristics of the three extended families

| | EVANS Socially and geographically immobile | | | MURROW Socially and geographically mobile | | | JACKSON Socially immobile and geographically mobile | | |
|---|---|---|---|---|---|---|---|---|---|
| | Alive | Dead | Total | Alive | Dead | Total | Alive | Dead | Total |
| Number of recognized kin | 145 | 57 | 202 | 41 | 10 | 51 | 66 | 14 | 80 |
| Number of households (excluding ego's) | 46 | | | 15 | | | 25 | | |
| *Geographical distribution* | | | | | | | | | |
| Within 25 miles | 119 ⎫ | | | — | | | — | | |
| Between 25–50 miles | 11 ⎬ 97·2% | | | — | | | — | | |
| 51–100 miles | 11 ⎭ | | | — | | | 9 | | |
| Over 100 miles | — | | | 41 = 100% | | | 51 ⎫ 86·4% | | |
| Abroad | 4 | | | — | | | 6 ⎭ | | |
| Total | 145 | | | 41 | | | 66 | | |
| *Household head's occupation* | | | | | | | | | |
| Manual | 5 = 10·8% | | | 12 = 80% | | | 4 = 16% | | |
| Non-manual | 41 = 89·2% | | | 3 = 20% | | | 21 = 84% | | |
| Total (in households) | 46 = 100% | | | 15 = 100% | | | 25 = 100% | | |

I have chosen three families each representing one combination of social and geographical mobility, rather than presenting one case study of a ceremonial happening (cf. Loudon's, 1961, study of a single funeral). It was not the ceremony or the happening in itself in which I was interested. Through a comparative study of three similar events each representing one variation of social and geographical mobility it is possible to develop the previously presented material on the structure and function of the middle class extended family. In doing this I follow Frankenberg (1966 (*a*)) on the importance of detailed studies of crises and ceremonial for a study of the underlying processes of industrial society. This approach is developed further in Chapter Seven.

So the detail of the following material can be justified because there is very little ethnographic material on the British middle class and secondly as a way of getting at the effects of social and geographical mobility on the strategic institution of the family.

For each family there is presented four genealogies, showing the composition of households, their geographical distribution, their manual/non-manual distribution and lastly concerned with the christening itself. Each family will be discussed in turn, beginning with the Evans, followed by the Jacksons and concluding with the Murrows. The four genealogies for each family form the basic data and for the sake of conciseness, I will not describe every link and every person mentioned but concentrate on those points relevant to my basic overall theme of social and geographical mobility.

## 2   The Evans Family

Robert Thomas, the son of John Evans an accountant (m.q. = 41) was christened in January at a Methodist Chapel. Over 100 kin were invited to attend either the chapel or the tea that followed, or both, and 96 in all came. This, in comparison to the Jackson and Murrow christenings, gives some indication of the size of the Evans kinship universe which in many ways is quite remarkable. Of the 32 complete genealogies that were collected, this was the largest, the most localized and the most middle class.

First I must make a caveat about this particular fieldwork

situation. The kinship information was collected from both John Evans and his wife, some interviews were separate but some were together and so the genealogy (and this point applies also to the Jackson and Murrow genealogies) very much represents the household's kinship universe. This is in line with Firth's finding that 'Husband and wife share their kin: they tend to act together in kin relations' (1956, p. 27). In the case of the Evans family, as the genealogy showing the composition of households shows, Evans' father was a member of the Evans household. I never interviewed him formally nor asked him for kinship information directly. But because it took several long interviews to build up this complete genealogy over a period of several months it is very likely that I stimulated considerable interest in their kinship universe and that kinship became a topic of conversation far more than otherwise would have been the case. Consequently there has been some 'leakage' of kinship information to them about which perhaps otherwise they would not have known. Because of this 'leakage' the proportion of dead, but not forgotten, kin is higher for the Evans genealogy than for either the Jackson's or the Murrow's, or indeed for most of the other families from whom I systematically collected kinship information. This 'leakage' is emphasized both by the 'depth' of the kinship information on Mr. Evans' side and by the number of dead kin on that side.

The Evans extended family is in fact even more localized than the genealogy showing geographical distribution of kin suggests. Of the 145 live kin, 141 live in the British Isles (throughout this section I am referring to recognized kin: see the remarks in the methodological introduction), of these 141, 130 are living within 50 miles of Swansea, 119 are within 25 miles and 107 of these actually live within the County Borough boundaries. Just to emphasize the middle class nature of this extended family 95 of these live within Swansea west.

Even allowing for the 'leakage' from John Evans' father the size of this genealogy is remarkable. This is not a remnant of a classical kin grouping in an old urban area but that of a middle class household living on a new private housing estate. Its size is remarkable, not just because it was unexpected but also because John Evans is an only child and his wife is only one of four. It was impossible to come to anything like an accurate

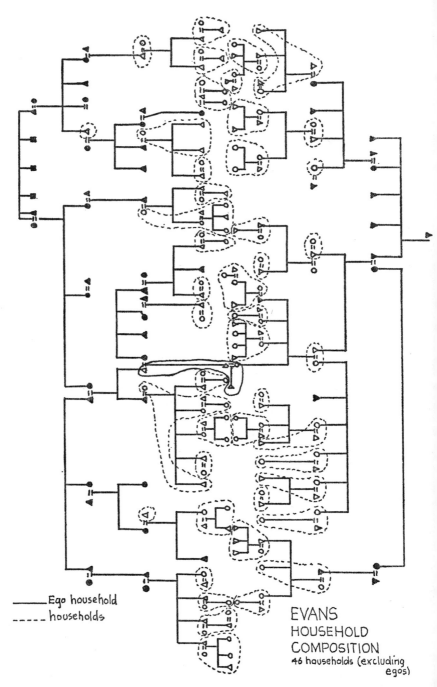

Ego household

households

EVANS
HOUSEHOLD
COMPOSITION
46 households (excluding
egos)

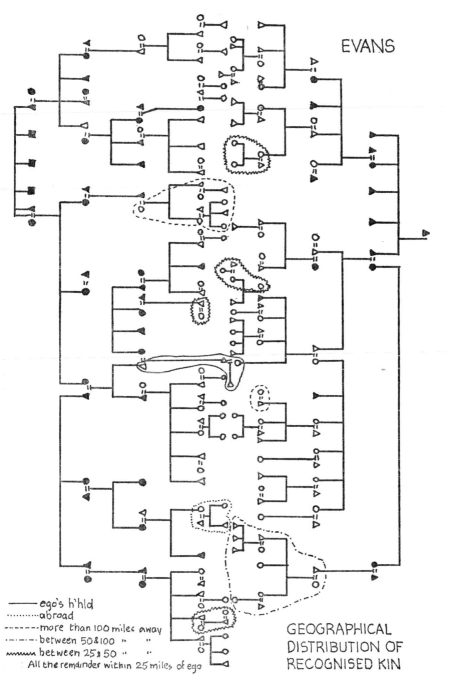

EVANS

GEOGRAPHICAL
DISTRIBUTION OF
RECOGNISED KIN

——— ego's h'hld
··········· abroad
------- more than 100 miles away
-·-·-·- between 50 & 100 "    "
wwwww between 25 & 50 "    "
All the remainder within 25 miles of ego

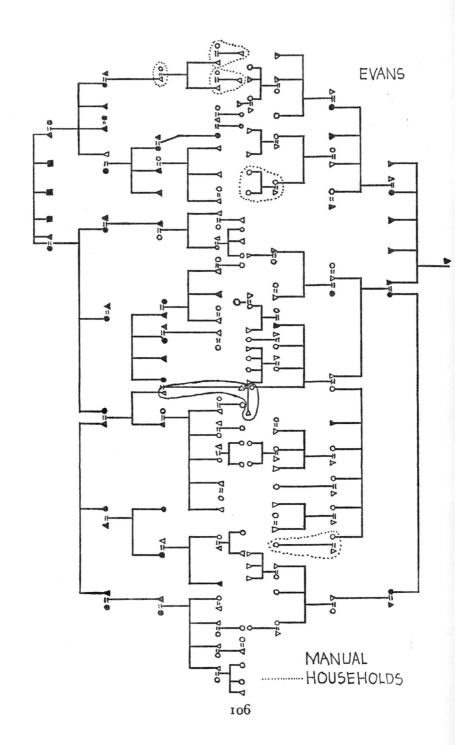

EVANS

MANUAL
·········· HOUSEHOLDS

106

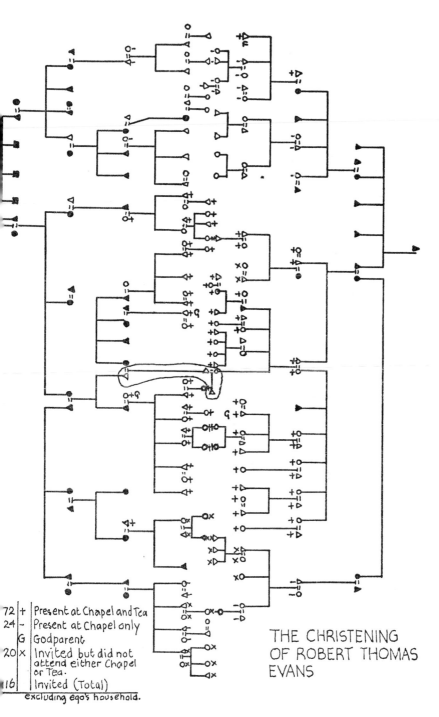

| 72 | + | Present at Chapel and Tea |
| 24 | − | Present at Chapel only |
|  | G | Godparent |
| 20 | x | Invited but did not attend either Chapel or Tea. |
| 16 |  | Invited (Total) |

excluding ego's household.

THE CHRISTENING
OF ROBERT THOMAS
EVANS

measure of the contact between different members of this extended family. Excluding the christening, the household I studied had seen over 100 relatives in the last six months, many of them many times. This is, of course, in marked contrast to both the Jacksons and the Murrows (see below) and is a reflection of the localized nature of the Evans kinship universe. So much so that both 'sides' knew each other well. For example John Evans' best man (marked F. on the last genealogy) was in fact Evans' wife's father's, father's, sister's, daughter's, son (W.F.F.Z.D.S): he was thought of as a cousin (this compares interestingly with the Jacksons, but contrasts with the Murrows).

The christening was stage managed by Mrs. Evans' mother. To emphasize the kin nature of the ceremony, they returned to Mrs. Evans' mother's for tea not to the Evans' house on the estate. Admittedly there would have been less room at the Evans' own house on the estate but as Mrs. Evans said, 'It's not that I don't like my neighbours but this was an occasion for the family, and if we had come back here I should have at least to have invited some of them' (compare the situation at the Murrows christening where no kin were invited).

Although all 116 invited could have got into the chapel, not all could have got into Mrs. Evans' parents' house. Only 72 of the 96 who accepted the invitations went to the tea *and* the chapel. (This caused insuperable difficulties in analysis because some went to the chapel and not the tea because they had very young children, and some came to the tea and not the chapel for precisely the same reason.) So attendance at both chapel and tea was not just a function of kinship position but also of stage in the family cycle.

In fact those invited illustrate, even where kin are as localized as in the Evans family, the ability of the middle class to choose the kin with whom they want to associate. It is necessary, to distinguish between those the Evans normally associate with and those Mrs. Evans' mother wanted to invite. The invitation list was based on the wedding invitation list (18 months earlier) with non-kin specifically excluded. As far as I could ascertain there were no non-kin at all at either chapel or tea, except those engaged to kin or those expected to become engaged. The Evans had complete freedom about whom they chose as godparents, but the kin gathering itself was organized by Mrs.

Evans' mother. It was she who sent out the invitations, the list being given to Evans' father for comments (he did not in fact alter it in any way).

One godfather was a cousin of Evans (mother's sister's son) who now lived in Cardiff, but had only recently moved away from Swansea. He was an insurance broker. He was the same age as Evans and they had been at school with each other (a minor public school in the Midlands). The two families, the Evanses and his cousins had been abroad on holiday together the previous summer. The second godfather was also a cousin (wife's mother's sister's son). A great deal was seen of him: indeed I thought for a long time he was a friend and not a relative (these divisions are in many ways false). Three weeks before the christening he moved to London. He was in banking. Evans and he played cricket regularly together. The choice of the third godparent seems a little strange: she was an aunt of Mr. Evans (father's brother's wife), an elderly lady who cannot really be expected to live long enough to perform her duties as a godparent. Her husband (Evans' father's brother) before he died was a partner of Evans' father. They were accountants, and Evans himself was now a partner in this firm.

It is significant that both godfathers had recently left the very localized kinship system. It is as if the godparenthood was conferred on them because they had left. It is in this context that it is interesting to note that all the kin living over 100 miles away but in the British Isles came to the christening but not all those living locally came. The one household that lived abroad (in Australia) were also invited 'so that they still felt part of the family'.

It will be seen from the genealogies that of the 46 households in the Evans extended family there were only five where the household head was in a manual occupation, four of these lived in Swansea. The fifth (wife's father's father's sister's son's daughter's family) 'works on the buses in the Rhondda—we don't know them'. But her parents and aunts attended the chapel. (F. who is genealogically as remote, attended as a friend, and his friendship with Evans has strengthened the kinship ties with his father—who came to both chapel and tea because he was F.'s father not because he was Mrs. Evans' F.F.Z.D.'s husband.) Of the three manual households on Mr.

Evans' side one attended the chapel but two, the households of the children of the first, did not. The manual household that attended was extremely genealogically remote, Mr. Evans' M.M.F.B.D. son's household. He was a retired tinplate worker, but a deacon at Evans' chapel. The only manual household that attended both the chapel and tea was that of Mrs. Evans' mother's sister. They lived in a council house in western Swansea and he worked for British Railways. Mrs. Evans said, 'Well she's my aunt and I like them anyway, salt of the earth'. Outside of kin gatherings such as this they were never seen by the Evans family.

Unlike the accounts of the Jackson and Murrow christenings that follow, my informants could not give me sufficient information about seating arrangements either in the chapel or at the tea. But the genealogy concerned with the christening does indicate who came to the chapel or the tea, or both. My information about gifts is however fuller. This is fortunate because a christening is an approved occasion for aid to be given to members of the middle class extended family.

Both grandfathers gave substantial sums of money via Mr. Evans to young Robert Thomas (between £500 and £1,000) to be 'put away' for him. This is understandable in the case of his paternal grandfather as Robert Thomas was his first grandchild. In the case of his maternal grandparents, Robert Thomas was their ninth grandchild (and they already had one great grandchild). However Mrs. Evans' father was undoubtedly a very wealthy man; he was a large wholesaler (note that both grandfathers had spent their entire working lives in the town of Swansea).

An interesting feature of the Evans genealogy should be pointed out, the lack of any parents for Mrs. Evans' mother. Throughout the fieldwork it was absolutely impossible to gain any information about them, all knowledge was always denied. This may be one reason for Mrs. Evans' mother's obvious pride and knowledge of the kinship universe into which she had married. It will be remembered that it was she, not Mrs. Evans that stage managed the christening. This lack of maternal grandparents emphasized a characteristic of all the genealogies that were collected, their lack of depth when compared to their width. But an analysis of aid between members of those middle class extended families is in opposition to this. Knowledge and recognition leads one to stress width rather than depth, but aid leads one to stress the relationship between ascendent and descendent kin and affinal kin rather than collateral kin, i.e. in terms of aid, parents and children and in-laws are more important than cousins, aunts and uncles.

The large gifts given by grandparents have already been mentioned. The point can be made when these gifts are compared to those of collateral kin. As far as I could ascertain all those invited sent or brought a small gift. The emphasis is on small: they were clothes and toys, and very much on the token level (the only other gift of money, not counting the godparents who will be dealt with below, was £10 from the household in Australia). The small gifts came however in large quantities because of the number of givers. As Mrs. Evans said, 'there are enough clothes to keep Dr. Barnardo's going for years'. The godparents however gave special gifts. This was usual in all the christenings for which I have collected information. The widow of Mr. Evans' father's brother gave a cheque for £100. The other two godparents, the cousins, were more conventional, giving an inscribed silver mug and an inscribed plaque (showing a view of Swansea).

The Evans christening was the extreme example of a kinship ceremony for a socially and geographically immobile family. Many of its characteristics were reproduced in other kin gatherings amongst the other 'local' families—both in size and in the exclusion of non-kin. I now pass to accounts of the Jackson and Murrow christenings, which contrast both with each other, and with the above account of the Evans christening.

## 3   The Jackson Family

The christening of Timothy Alan, son of Peter Jackson, took place in the local Anglican church one Sunday afternoon in March. He was the third child. Peter Jackson was a geographically mobile plant superintendent (m.q. = 45), he had previously worked in three other towns, none of them in Wales, and he expected to move within a 'couple of years'.

The christening was a small affair and largely a kin gathering, it was attended by seven kin outside the Jackson household. To emphasize the kin nature of the christening, the Jacksons' 'daily woman' who came to the church with her daughter was not invited to the tea after the christening. One godparent was not a kinsman and he and his family attended both the church and the tea. The non-kin godparent was a colleague of Jackson and also lived on the estate. He and his wife were quasi-kin to Jackson's two elder children. Similarly Jackson and his wife were quasi-kin to their two children.

As well as the seven kin who actually came, ten more were invited but did not come. All of the kin that came to the christening lived over 100 miles away and all were in non-manual occupations (or married to people in non-manual occupations). Jackson's father was a small town tradesman who had just retired, and his brother (who had very recently been killed in an accident) had been a teacher who had also been geographically mobile. Jackson and his dead brother's household and his parents did not live within 100 miles of each other. The small town in which his father had had a shop and in which he had been brought up was still thought of as home and was visited regularly.

Jacksons' niece was married to a doctor in London (she had been a nurse). She was invited with her husband but they were not expected to come. They did however send a christening present of a large cuddly toy. Jackson's nephew, who attended the christening, was at university. He came home from university especially to accompany his mother who was to be a godparent at the christening.

So on Jackson's side, his parents and the family of his dead brother were invited; and no others, although as the genealogy showing the geographical distribution of kin shows, there were others who lived closer. There was a great deal of gossip about these kin during the weekend of the christening. Jackson's father's dead brother's wife, who had remarried, lived in another South Wales town. Jackson's parents would not visit her, even though they drove through this town, because they had not been invited to her second marriage. Jackson had not invited them because his parents would not have wanted them to be invited. The Jacksons however saw his aunt and her second husband about once a month. The manual household that lived between

50 and 100 miles away were thought to be 'very rough'. Mrs. Jackson said, 'I could not have them here, it's not that I am a

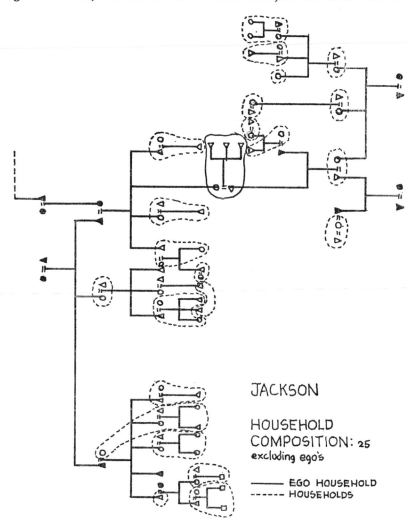

JACKSON

HOUSEHOLD
COMPOSITION: 25
excluding ego's

———— EGO HOUSEHOLD
------- HOUSEHOLDS

snob but we don't mix. He's a porter on the railway or something.' His supposed promiscuous habits were a great topic of conversation over the christening weekend.

On Mrs. Jackson's side, all her siblings and siblings-in-law and their children and their children's husbands were invited.

Mrs. Jackson's parents were both dead; her father had been a solicitor in the same small town as Jackson's father had had his shop. Mrs. Jackson's eldest brother, who was a godparent, had

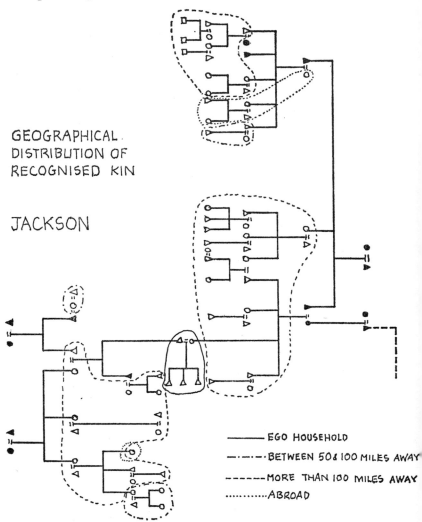

GEOGRAPHICAL
DISTRIBUTION OF
RECOGNISED KIN

JACKSON

——————— EGO HOUSEHOLD

—·—·—·— BETWEEN 50 & 100 MILES AWAY

— — — — MORE THAN 100 MILES AWAY

·············· ABROAD

gone into his father's firm. Over the weekend there was a good deal of banter between Jackson's father and Mrs. Jackson's eldest brother about the professions and the trades. Mrs. Jackson's eldest brother had two children. The older, a son, had

recently married, after graduating from Oxford and was now
in the junior managerial ranks of industry, working for an extremely large organization in Scotland. He and his wife were

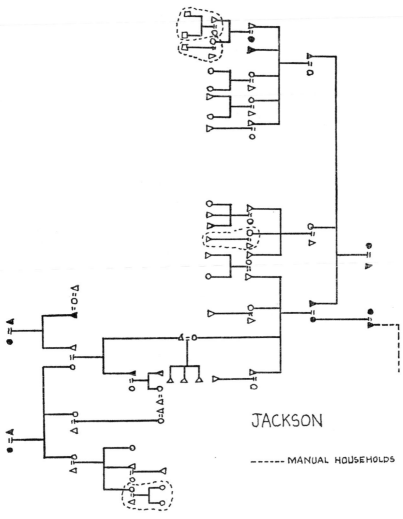

JACKSON

------ MANUAL HOUSEHOLDS

invited, but similarly to Jackson's recently married niece were
not really expected to attend, but they sent a card. Their
younger child, a daughter, came with her parents, she was in
her last year at a grammar school.

Mrs. Jackson's eldest sister is married to a regular army officer, stationed in the Home Counties. They and their son

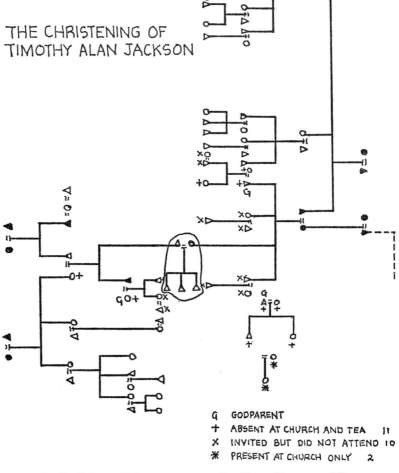

THE CHRISTENING OF
TIMOTHY ALAN JACKSON

G   GODPARENT
+   ABSENT AT CHURCH AND TEA   11
✗   INVITED BUT DID NOT ATTEND  10
✳   PRESENT AT CHURCH ONLY   2

were invited but did not come, pleading distance. They sent some clothes as a present. Her younger brother is an academic at a northern university and although he and his family were invited, he gave the same excuse as his eldest sister: distance. He and his wife sent a card.

So on both sides invitations were only extended to siblings and their families and parents (compare this with the Evans). Mrs. Jackson recognized as kin as far away as father's brother's son's son's child. As can be seen from the genealogy, Mrs Jackson did not know the sex of these children and in fact did not know the address of their parents.

Over the weekend of the christening, as all the kin came from over 100 miles away, accommodation had to be arranged. Jackson's parents came by car and stayed in the Jackson's house, as did his widowed sister-in-law and nephew. His parents arrived on the Friday and his sister-in-law on the Saturday. Both left after the tea on the Sunday. Mrs. Jackson's eldest brother and his family stayed with the colleague of Jackson's who lived on the estate and who was a godparent.

Although both sides of the family came from the same town there had been very little contact in the past. Jackson's father knew Mrs. Jackson's brother only slightly and had never met Mrs. Jackson's father (who had died before Jackson married). Jackson's dead brother had, as a child, known Mrs. Jackson's elder sister, both had moved away when they left school and had had no further contact.

Mrs. Jackson and her three siblings are a fine example of the differing geographical mobility to which the middle class is prone. Her brother would be a burgess in Watson's terminology and both herself and her sister had married spiralists. Her younger brother himself was at least a potential spiralist.

Within the core of Jackson's extended family represented by those invited to the christening there existed interlocking god-parent relationships. Jackson himself was godparent to both of his dead brother's children and Mrs. Jackson was godmother to her husband's brother's daughter. Mrs. Jackson was godmother to both her elder brother's children (neither her elder sister nor her younger brother had had their child christened). The godparents of the two elder Jackson children had been, for the eldest: Jackson's father and brother and sister-in-law, for the second child, Jackson's brother again, and Mrs. Jackson's elder brother and his wife.

All three godparents gave substantial presents. Mrs. Jackson's brother gave £100, and Jackson's sister gave £10. The third godparent, Jackson's colleague, gave an inscribed silver tankard. Jackson's father gave £50 as he had done to Jackson's two older children. So Timothy Alan Jackson at the age of 2½ months had a bank account of £160.

Over the weekend they naturally took every opportunity to

$$\boxed{\text{F}}$$

gf  gf  gm  f  m̊

ff  fm  pd  p  s  s

n  ne mbw  KwKsKs

The JACKSON
Christening

| F | Font |
|---|------|
| * | Timothy Alan |
| m | mother |
| f | father |
| gf | godfather |
| gm | godmother |
| p | Daily woman |
| d | daughter |
| s | son |
| n | nephew |
| ne | niece |
| K | colleague |
| w | wife |
| mbw | mother's brother's wife |

see each other and catch up on family and home town gossip (on the Saturday evening Jackson's brother's son took Mrs. Jackson's brother's daughter to the pictures—about which there was a great deal of teasing and speculation). But there was none of the grouping that was observable at the Evans christening.

At the christening itself the 'daily woman' was introduced to the kin that she had not previously met, i.e. Mrs. Jackson's brother's family. The diagram above shows the seating in the church, Mrs. Jones the 'daily woman' being invaluable for keeping the two elder Jackson children quiet. The three god-parents, plus the parents sat in the pew nearest the font; behind them sat Jackson's parents, the daily woman and her daughter and the Jacksons' two elder children. In the third row sat Jackson's nephew, Mrs. Jackson's niece and her mother, the wife of Jackson's colleague, who was a godparent, and her two children.

The Jacksons' kinship universe had a well defined core, all of whom were invited to the christening, but beyond this they were most certainly in the words of Mrs. Jackson 'second rank' and 'those we don't bother with'. For these geographically mobile members of the middle class the christening was an opportunity to gather and to see one another. To emphasize this mobility the third godparent was not a kinsman. Even so the christening was primarily a kin occasion. Despite the distances between households, the warmth of the meeting, and the ex-change of gifts at least point to the danger of defining out of 'the extended family' such kin groups who are not in almost daily contact. (See discussion in Chapter Four.) Also the Jacksons' extended family shows that aid flows through the male link and that amongst the geographically mobile it somewhat overshadows the previously emphasized mother–daughter link.

## 4   *The Murrow Family*

Kevin Leyton Murrow was the first child of Paul Murrow, a civil engineer with a m.q. of 48·3. Not only had the Murrows been extremely geographically mobile but both husband and wife had been socially mobile. They had been married for seven years. Murrow's father was an agricultural labourer and his wife's father was a 'fitter' in a large engineering works in a Midland town. He and his wife had initially been socially mobile through the education system, through local grammar schools and university. They met at their provincial university, where he read applied science and she English. Before the birth of Kevin she had taught in infant schools.

The Murrow christening was in fact held in the same church as that of the Jacksons, but unlike both the Jackson and the Evans was not attended by any kin whatsoever outside the

Murrow household. No kin were invited on the presumption that they could not afford to come and so there would be little point in inviting them.

Kevin's godparents were his parents and Mr. Owen who worked with Mr. Murrow. Also present at the church were Owen's fiancée and Mr. and Mrs. Lincoln who were neighbours from the estate (three doors away, and had also been socially and geographically mobile). So the christening was attended by seven people including Kevin. All went back to the Murrows for tea afterwards. The seating at the church is shown in the diagram below.

The MURROW
Christening

| | |
|---|---|
| F | Font |
| * | Kevin Leyton |
| gf | godfather |
| gm | godmother |
| O | Owen's-fiancée |
| L | Lincoln |
| W | wife |

Although no kin were invited to the christening they were still seen at other times. As Mrs. Murrow's mother lived in the Midlands with her unmarried sister and Mr. Murrow's parents lived in the West Country, they were not seen very often: about twice a year. Neither parental household owned a car. Both of Murrow's father's brothers were (or had been) agricultural workers and so were three of his cousins. On the other hand the daughter of his father's second eldest brother had married an 'insurance man' (see genealogy showing manual/non-manual distribution) and was thought to have done very well for herself. But not as well as the Murrows' family's pride and joy: Mr. Murrow himself. 'They are proud of me, I send them pictures of things I am building and my pa takes them down the local.' 'When I go home I get taken round like a prize pig—I am still the only one, as far as I know, from my family who has ever gone to university.' The Murrows will take Kevin home in the summer to the

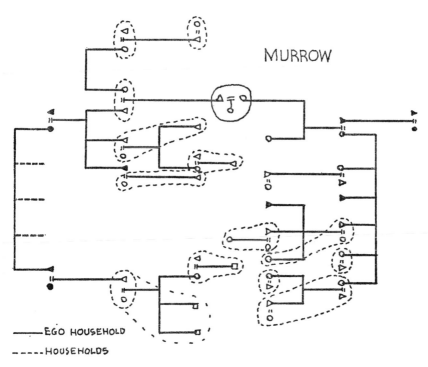

MURROW

——— EGO HOUSEHOLD
- - - - - HOUSEHOLDS

## HOUSEHOLD COMPOSITION
### 15 HOUSEHOLDS (EXCLUDING EGO'S)

West Country 'but it is difficult because there is not room for us to stay really'.

On Mrs. Murrow's side the only kin about whom she knew were the siblings of her mother. Of these seven households, six were manual. The seventh was a clerk in the 'co-op'. They all still lived in the same town as her mother, but neither her mother nor Mrs. Murrow herself had any contact, beyond Christmas cards. Mrs. Murrow said 'I wouldn't even know about them if it weren't for Mum.'

Compared with other households on both sides the Murrows had done well, but the Murrows were a good example of the situation of the geographically and socially mobile member of the middle class. Participation in the christening highlights this situation. Whereas both the Evans and the Jacksons received substantial gifts at their christening, the Murrows did not.

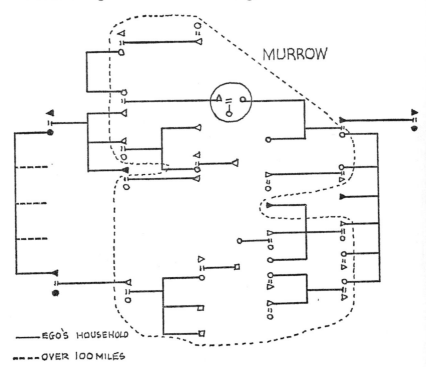

GEOGRAPHICAL DISTRIBUTION
OF RECOGNISED KIN

Although they did not invite members of their family to Kevin's christening they did tell their parents in advance about it. And the Murrows received vastly elaborate christening cards from Mr. Murrow's parents, mother's sister's and father's brothers' and two cousins' households. (All six in fact.) They had not told any other household but Mr. Murrow's parents and Mrs. Murrow's mother told the others—an indication of the close-knit kin network that he had left behind. Murrow's parents also sent a coat for the child and Mrs. Murrow said that they would have to take a photograph of Kevin in it because he would be too big for it by the summer when they would take him to see his paternal grandparents.

Mrs. Murrow's mother sent a letter about ten days later hoping that the christening had gone well, but neither card nor

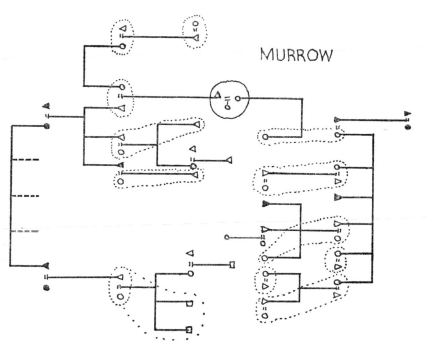

MURROW

MANUAL HOUSEHOLDS

present. This caused no comment. Indeed the Murrows seemed a little embarrassed by the number of cards that they had received from Mr. Murrow's side.

There is one striking similarity between the Murrow christening and the Evans christening and this is the segregation of kin and non-kin, but in opposite ways. The Evans christening is remarkable for the exclusion of all non-kin whereas at the Murrow christening no kin were present at all. Neither Mr. Owen nor the Lincolns (both present at the Murrow christening) had ever met any of the Murrows kinship universe. The

difference in the kinship universe of a family that has been socially
and geographically immobile and one that has been socially and

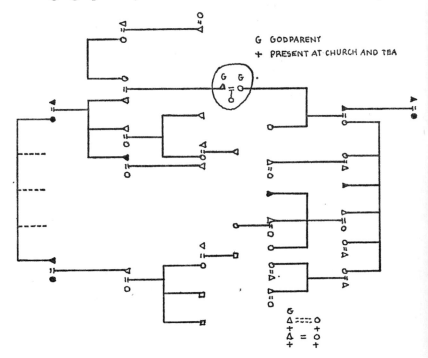

G GODPARENT

+ PRESENT AT CHURCH AND TEA

## THE CHRISTENING OF
## KEVIN LEYTON MURROW

geographically mobile could not be more explicit than in a
comparison of the Evans and Murrow christenings.

### 5  *Conclusions*

By concentrating on one ceremonial occasion for three families
with different mobility experience some aspects of the structure
and function of the middle class extended family have been
highlighted. Table 5:5 summarizes the basic characteristics of
the three christenings that have been analysed above.

During the fieldwork I collected complete data on eleven
christenings: one only for a local family—the Evans, six for the

TABLE 5:5   *Summary of characteristics of the three christenings*

|  | EVANS: $m.q. = 41$ | | | JACKSON: $m.q. = 45$ | | | MURROW: $m.q. = 48·3$ | | |
|---|---|---|---|---|---|---|---|---|---|
|  | Kin | Non-kin | Total | Kin | Non-kin | Total | Kin | Non-kin | Total |
| Number invited | 116* | — | 116 | 17 | 6 | 23 | — | 4 | 4 |
| Number who came† | 96 | — | 96 | 7 | 6 | 12 | — | 4 | 4 |

\* Including fiancées as kin.
† To church/chapel and/or tea.

geographically and socially mobile and four for the geographically mobile but socially immobile. The average attendance not including the members of the household studied for the ten geographically mobile was nine (compared to seven in Bethnal Green (Young and Willmott: 1957, p. 85)). The average for those who had been both geographically and socially mobile was 7·6 people (cf. Murrow four), and for the non-locals from middle class backgrounds, 11 (cf. Jackson 13). As stressed earlier the Evans were in every way exceptional.

The significance of the christening for the Evans perhaps can be summed up by Mrs. Evans who said, 'I don't know why we bother it is only for the family.' But for the Murrows, kin were not invited. It is significant that all non-kin invited to these three christenings came, but not all kin who were invited were expected to come. Although the invitations must be seen as one way of keeping other kin up to date in kin affairs. They received their invitations by virtue of their kinship position, whereas non-kin were chosen for themselves. In the case of the Evans the kin universe was large enough and diverse enough for Evans to choose with whom he wanted to be friendly, although his mother-in-law used the occasion it would seem to assemble as many kin together as possible. For the Evans, less so for the Jacksons and not at all for the Murrows, the genealogy can provide a frame of reference, both in time and space to which a great deal of day-to-day and week-to-week social activity may be related.

Frankenberg interpreting Young and Willmott's kinship material from Bethnal Green says of christenings that 'this particular ceremony re-emphasizes and yet makes more limited the uniting of kindreds which a wedding brings about' (1966 (*b*), p. 191). This obviously was meant to apply only to the working class situation. However it would be also true of the Jacksons, and I would suggest from an examination of other kin gatherings of local families, of the non-mobile but not the Evans. For the Evans the christening was an occasion to emphasize the size of their kinship universe. For the Murrows it was an occasion to, if anything, emphasize their isolation from their wider kindred and to symbolically draw closer to both their neighbours and his colleagues.

The comparison of these three christenings also underlines the themes of the previous chapter. That any consideration of social mobility must not neglect extended family aid, and that this aid must of necessity vary in both quantity and quality between those who have been socially mobile and those who come from middle class backgrounds, and between those who have been geographically mobile and those who have been both born and bred locally. An analysis of this aid leads to a stressing of the ascendent and descendent and affinal kin at the expense of collateral kin, and that it is the male aspects of this structure through which aid flows, and that their importance has been overshadowed by the stress laid upon the mother–married daughter link resulting from studies of old working class areas characterized by low rates of social and geographical mobility.

CHAPTER SIX

# The Estates

## 1  *Introduction*

In this country what the poet Philip Larkin has called 'the mortgaged half-built fringes' of towns have not attracted much serious sociological attention. These 'green ghettoes dedicated to the elite and segregated by class and space' (Mumford: 1963, p. 493) have largely continued to be successful in their 'collective attempt to lead a private life' (Mumford: 1946, p. 213). This is not the case in North America where suburbia has attracted a great deal of attention both from the 'commentators' and by the 'scientists', to use Dobriner's distinction.

The difficulties of research into family life in suburbia has been well put by that sensitive observer, Molly Harrington, when she wrote: 'the variety and range of family and neighbourhood patterns found in the newer districts may be seen less as a tangled web to be unravelled than as an example of the diversity of human behaviour when the rigid framework of physical necessity is loosened and personal choice is a major determinant of life style' (1965, p. 136). And it was just this diversity that this researcher found most difficult, even more so as most of the previous literature, which is summarized in the first section of this chapter, stressed the homogeneity of suburbia. I found the techniques used by previous workers of little value in this study of social and geographical mobility amongst 120 middle class families living on two private housing estates. The next section of this chapter is about participation on the estate and also analyses gossip.

My problem was how to study the process of social mobility

on two middle class housing estates. Frankenberg has recently and pointedly stressed the difficulties of the anthropologist who wants to study process in modern urban society:

'When I went to Glynceirog I was always conscious of my anthropological colleagues' anecdotes of how they sat in the centre of African villages while life went on around them and encompassed them. They could not avoid becoming part of the social processes they wished to observe. In my early days in the village I would often climb a hill and look sadly down upon the rows of houses of the housing estate and wonder what went on inside them . . . had I studied Bethnal Green or the Sheffield housing estate the observation of social process would have presented ever greater difficulties . . . students of areas of this kind try to devise techniques to get over this problem. By and large, however, they can only deduce social process from the information they can collect by questioning people in their homes or elsewhere. For there are no activities which concern the estate as a whole' (1966 (*b*), p. 16).

There is a way out of these difficulties by focusing on dramatic occurrences. In the previous chapter, on the family, I concluded with detailed accounts of three christenings which illuminated the effects of the processes of social and geographical mobility on the family. In the next chapter there is a detailed account of one incident on the larger of the two estates studied which illuminates the effects of the processes of social and geographical mobility on the structure of social relations on that estate. This case study of a single happening is used to articulate much of the previous material. Such an approach is novel as far as I know in this environment.

There is one major limitation to the following discussion of social relationships on the two estates. To a great extent it ignores the children, of whom there were 258 at the first count. In analysing the patterns of social relationships on the two estates, those relating to children were not pursued specifically: it would have been beyond the scope of a single fieldworker. As already emphasized the estates were not studied for themselves but for the data they would yield on the effects of social and geographical mobility.

A survey of the previous literature on suburban social relations reveals that there have in the past been three major approaches. These I shall call; firstly, the 'macro-ecological' within which are included those works that use class as a major variable; secondly there are the 'micro-ecological' studies; and thirdly there is what I call the 'sequential'. I shall discuss each approach in turn.

The ecological segregation of towns is now very well documented (see Collison and Mogey: 1959, Williams and Herbert: 1963). In the sphere of private housing, with which I am concerned here, it can be argued that the prices of the houses act as a social sieve, with graduated meshes as it were, through which drop each homogeneous segment of the population round the edge of towns. Pahl has noted that 'there is a tendency in England at the moment for people to move to estates which are dominated by people of similar socio-economic status' (1965, p. 19). The geographically mobile members of the middle class move from one spatially segregated estate to another where they settle among people of similar wealth and status.

The facts of ecological segregation by class and status cannot be disputed but as Watson noted, both spiralists and burgesses are often neighbours (1964, p. 151). It is just this fact that is largely ignored by the macro-ecologists. There *is* ecological segregation by class and status but within the middle class there are very different groups whose existence must be acknowledged to make sense of the social relations on the estate.

Martin claimed for suburbia two defining characteristics, firstly their ecological relationship to the rest of the community, and secondly their high rate of commuting. From these two major characteristics he argues that there are three derivative factors:

(*a*) homogeneity,

(*b*) a high rate of informal interaction and formal participation,

(*c*) a set of suburban socio-economic characteristics from selective in-migration to the suburbs.

Perhaps the key to Martin's thinking is contained in the title to his paper: 'The Structuring of Social Relationships *Engendered* by Suburban Residence' (my emphasis). The empirical data that I collected will not support Martin's thesis; suburban residence is only one and a relatively minor factor in the 'structuring' of social relationships. Indeed most of the social relationships of the 120 families that I studied can be explained without recourse to the factor of suburban residence.

Similarly Fava paraphrasing Wirth, in her 'Suburbanism as a Way of Life' (1956) claimed that suburbs were characterized by three features:

(a) a disproportionate share of young married couples and therefore a dominance of reproductive and child socialization functions,

(b) middle-classness, therefore they are a 'second melting pot' for the socially mobile,

(c) open nature.

The first characteristic is common to most new housing, not just suburbia and among the 120 families studied 67% were in the child rearing stage. On the second characteristic, only just over 25% of the families had been socially mobile. It could therefore be argued that both of Fava's first two features were present, but they did not help really in a study of the effects of social and geographical mobility. The third feature—that of the open nature of suburbia—I will be concerned with under the heading of 'micro-ecology'.

Dobriner (1963) is one of the most important and sensible writers on suburbia, serving as a palliative to both the crude macro-ecology described above and to the wilder 'commentators'. He, like Berger (1960, 1961) stresses the centrality of class as a variable in explaining suburban behaviour, and explores the question of how much suburban life styles, behaviour and social structure are due to their unique ecological position and how much is really another subtle manifestation of social class. After a survey of the literature Dobriner reduces suburbia to five main variables:

(a) their ecological position,

(b) commuting,

(c) their middle class nature,

(d) homogeneity,

(e) visibility.

The two estates that I studied are both firmly embedded in the urban fabric of western Swansea and have no different ecological position than a great deal of the rest of the town, including the new council housing. They are both emphatically not commuting suburbs as the table below giving place of work shows.

TABLE 6:1

| Place of husbands' work | Number | | |
|---|---|---|---|
| Swansea County Borough: | | | |
| West | 18 | | |
| East | 29 | | |
| Central Business District | 22 | Total | 69 |
| Coast | | | 22 |
| Industrial Carmarthen | | | 10 |
| Swansea Valley | | | 3 |
| Neath Valley | | | 2 |
| Further away | | | 4 |
| No specific area | | | 6 |
| Retired | | | 4 |
| | | Total | 120 |

Both the estates are very clearly demarcated and distinct from place of work. 64 husbands come home to lunch regularly. There is however a very noticeable tendency for non-locals to be prepared to travel much greater distances to work than the locals. Of the 47 husbands who work outside the county borough, 41 are non-locals. Of the 18 occupied locals living on the two estates, 12 work within the county borough. As regards Dobriner's third variable, both estates are inhabited by people that could be called middle class by any of the usual criteria used to place people. But I cannot agree with the fourth variable, that of homogeneity because one of the major conclusions of this thesis is the marked difference in participation by different groups on the two estates. This is related to differing experience and expectation of geographical mobility. It is to the fifth factor of 'visibility' that I turn now and would want to widen to include all the 'micro-ecological' variables. e.g. Part seven of Whyte's *The Organization Man* (1956).

The classic micro-ecological study is that of Festinger, Schacter and Back: *Social Pressures in Informal Groups*, subtitled 'a study of human factors in housing'. Their study is of the relationship between group formation and micro-ecological factors. As they themselves wrote, these micro-ecological factors will make themselves most strongly felt where the community is homogeneous (1951, p. 161). The same spatial influence was found earlier by Merton (1943) and this whole ecological approach has since been widely utilized in the United States.

For example, from a study of small housing development Form (1945) makes the micro-ecological hypothesis of 'the principle of least effort' which he elaborates to be 'those people who reside closest to each other in terms of distance, physical orientation or accessibility tend to become friends or form close knit units'. Whyte in his analysis of social relations in Park Forest, home of *The Organization Man* wrote, 'we went into every other factor that could provide for the friendship patterns . . . just as the resident had said, it was the layout that was the major factor' (1956, p. 314).

Caplow and Forman (1950) in a study of 50 dwelling units advance beyond a reliance upon micro-ecological variables and include what they call 'community-structure', by which they mean cliques and groups. A much more sophisticated discussion is that of Gans who wrote that '. . . while physical proximity does affect some visiting patterns, positive relationships with neighbours and the more intensive forms of social interaction, such as friendship, require homogeneity of background, or of interests, or of values' (1961, p. 134). Proximity is not enough to create intensive relationships, even though it may well initiate some relations and maintain less intensive ones: i.e. proximity may be the initial cause of a relationship on an estate but cannot be a final or sufficient cause. Professor Sprott is right when he writes 'the siting of houses is by no means unimportant, but of greater importance are the attitudes, habits and aspirations of the people who live in them' (1958, p. 98).

The data presented later in this chapter will support this. After a long period of struggling I abandoned any attempt at a micro-ecological explanation of social relationships on the estates. As Festinger *et al.* wrote in their above cited Westgate study: 'if marked differences in background and interest among the residents had existed, these differences might have been so important as to overwhelm and obscure other determinants of group formation and social process' (1951, p. 9). It was just these 'marked differences', particularly of mobility experience that led to the eventual abandonment of micro-ecological analysis on both estates.

One major weakness of the micro-ecological approach is that

it does not adequately cater for the dynamic aspects of social relations. However, there is a third approach that does. It is called the 'sequential' approach. Mowrer hypothesized a sequence of suburban social relations, from 'home-centredness' and 'primary-group neighbourliness' to 'individualization' and 'community relations'. The first stage, that of 'pioneering', is when status signs are forgotten in the myriad of tasks involving the establishment of a new home in a new area in which the physical surroundings are not yet conquered (by which he means that the lawns are not yet laid). This stage is character-ized by primary group relations. The second stage is that during which cliques develop in terms of occupational interests. During the third stage both husband and wife reorientate their interests towards the wider community and away from the neighbour-hood (Mowrer: 1961).

There are objections that can be made to the sequential approach. Firstly it assumes a remarkable stability of population, when in fact in most new housing developments there is a high annual turnover: on the two estates studied there was in the year from when I began fieldwork a 24% turnover. (Whyte claimed for Park Forest an annual turnover of approximately 33%.) Ruth Durant's classic description of Watling as 'not much more than a huge hotel without a roof; the constant turnover of its population is the greatest single handicap to its development into a community' (1939, p. 119 makes the same point). How-ever there is some empirical evidence to support the sequential hypothesis. Dobriner wrote of Levittown:

> older residents recall more intense neighbouring in the first few years. At this time a 'pioneer spirit' prevailed and there existed a strong 'consciousness of kind' based on the sharing of a novel and intimate experience, the founding of a neighbourhood and a community. As the years went by however and as families moved away and new ones took their place, the early solidarity and spontaneous cliquing gave way to greater formality and social isolation (1963, p. 136).

From my fieldwork I would suggest however that a proportion of the estate population was 'community orientated' through-out, not just after several years. This was particularly true of those I have termed locals or burgesses.

In this country Morris and Mogey (1965) have put forward a very similar 'phase hypothesis' for the development of social relations, based on their study of a new council estate. In the first six months the estate had what they called an 'unfurnished atmosphere' and social relations were characterized by friendliness. A second stage begins when, due to the increase in the size of the estate it is impossible to know everybody else, and this stage grades into the next when breaches occur because common problems appear less important and social differences between residents become more apparent and frictions more difficult to contain. In the particular situation that I studied, although there was not the same increase in size as in the estate studied by Morris and Mogey, there was however a greater transience and turnover of population which it could be argued had the same effect.

It is possible to combine the second and third approaches and argue that micro-ecological variables as discussed above would be most important in the first stage of the cycle of suburban relations and that they steadily decrease in importance through the second stage, until they are no longer of any importance in the third stage. For this sequential approach to be used it is really necessary to study the development of social relations from the beginning, as Morris and Mogey were able to do, but I was not. It would have been necessary for me to rely to a far greater extent that I was prepared on what Sorokin somewhat contemptuously calls 'hear-say stuff'. I consequently abandoned both the macro- and micro-ecological approaches and then the sequential approach.

I thought that it might have been possible to construct scales of social distance (Borgardus: 1928, 1933, and Banton: 1960), although any scale of social distance for a middle class housing estate would have a very short distance from end to end compared to the original Borgardus scale. I thought careful interviewing and observation would make it possible to specify relationships more closely spaced than the Borgardus' seven. Banton has argued that the attempt is worthwhile and for a while social distance was a straw to be grasped at as I went down for a third time in a morass of field data. I eventually gave up the attempt to construct scales of social distance not because I did not think it worthwhile but because I decided that there were other solutions to my problem, and these are drawn more from social anthropology.

## 2  *Participation and Gossip*

At the end of Chapter Three the effects of social and geographical mobility on friendship was examined and it was pointed out that non-locals are far more dependent upon the estates for day-to-day contacts and as a source of friends than are the locals. In Chapter Four it was shown that locals tended also to have other local kin, in contrast to the non-locals.

An examination of the field data on the friendship patterns of the 120 wives suggests the hypothesis that the estates perform different functions for the geographically mobile than for the locals. Indeed it was not uncommon for those who had been geographically mobile to say that one reason for moving on to the estate when they came to Swansea, was that it would be easier to get to know people because there would be others 'in the same boat'. A wife of a geographically mobile but socially immobile insurance man (m.q. = 46) specifically contrasted the situation in another town where they had lived in a longer established middle class neighbourhood where it had been 'terribly difficult to find anyone to talk to—they didn't want to know'.

The locals however did not make the same investment in the social relations of the estate. They had other friends locally (not to mention kin) and so did not have as great a need for the estate to provide day-to-day contact. Those functions which kin are described as performing in old established working class areas such as Bethnal Green, for the non-locals are often performed by neighbours. As Klein has written 'a young married couple of the highly mobile kind would not be living near parents just at that time when they needed them most, during confinements, for baby-sitting, to help with shopping when children are small, nursing babies through illness and so on' (1965, p. 334). This is not the case for the locals. They could still call upon local extra-estate friends and kin for aid and assistance.

As in any other similar situation, the relationships between the housewives on the estate was based to a very great extent on reciprocation: baby-sitting was exchanged, a group of husbands got together to help lay each other's drives. It is to the advantage of the non-locals to reciprocate these services and to create obligations. The locals on the other hand had no such need: children could be left with their grandparents or two brothers could come up one weekend and lay the garage drive. The friendship cliques that formed after the initial 'pioneering' stage (see previous section in this chapter) consisted either of all locals or all non-locals.

In the words of a local (wife of a dentist, m.q. 34·5)

> I found that they were always dropping in offering to baby-sit and her husband came round with his "rota-digger" to have a go at the back garden without being asked. I didn't particularly want them to baby-sit, my sister always does and anyway they were only so keen, so we would offer to baby-sit for them and things like that—not that I blame them or anything and they are very nice people but honestly we don't *need* them (my emphasis).

Thus it can be seen that need is the key to a great deal of the social relations on the two estates. A non-local, wife of an academic (m.q. 48) said,

> I don't know what I would do without them—Sally and Jill I mean, they are just like me, they've come from away as well and we help each other. Taking it in turn to look after the children so that one of us can go into town unencumbered, and it's the same in the evening—without them I don't think we would ever get out.

Because the local families did not *need* to become so deeply involved in the estate social relations they showed a reluctance to do so. On both estates the local families had a reputation varying from being shy, through being 'a bit standoffish' to being 'downright bloody unfriendly'. The locals on both estates were known as 'The Welsh'. This in fact is not strictly fair because some non-locals were also Welsh from other parts of Wales and some locals were not very Welsh (see Appendix C). In the words of a non-local, wife of an engineer (m.q. 45):

> they don't really want to get to know you, have you noticed that, it's as if you are unwelcome in their country, no I don't mean that, they are just different and they keep themselves to themselves, not like (and here she listed five families, all non-locals) we all know each other very well, I wouldn't really call

them friends, not what I call friends, but they will do things for you. Not like the Welsh. I hope you don't think I am being unfair but there it is, they just don't *join in* like the rest of us (my emphasis).

From the introduction on methods it will be remembered that a dozen informants were asked to keep a dairy for me, about whom they met. The edited extracts from two diaries will do two things, firstly show the difference in the kind of interaction between the locals and the non-locals on the estates and secondly and more tentatively perform for the wives what the two career biographies did in Chapter Two of the book, i.e. give the flavour of the middle class way of life.

The two extracts that follow are both for the same week in March. The details about household activity have been edited out and so really what is given below is a list of the people with whom these two women interacted in a week.

Mrs. M. is the wife of a local solicitor with a m.q. of 38 and Mrs. J. is the wife of an operations research engineer with a m.q. of 47·5. Both have two small pre-school age children.

*Mrs. M.* (local)

| | | |
|---|---|---|
| Saturday: | a.m. | Met father-in-law while shopping. |
| | p.m. | Cousin (Mr. M.'s father's brother's second son) and his wife called in during the evening. |
| Sunday: | a.m. | |
| | p.m. | Niece called (elder sister's eldest child) and two extra estate friends called. |
| | | In evening went to play bridge with two other extra estate friends. |
| | | (Mrs. M.'s mother babysat.) |
| Monday: | a.m. | |
| | p.m. | Spent afternoon with mother. |
| Wednesday: | a.m. | Spent all day with mother. |
| | p.m. | In evening went to meeting with her mother, niece babysat. |
| Thursday: | a.m. | |
| | p.m. | In evening uncle and aunt called (Mrs. M.'s mother's sister and husband). |
| Friday: | a.m. | |
| | p.m. | In afternoon went shopping with mother. |

*Mrs. J.* (non-local)

| | | |
|---|---|---|
| Saturday: | a.m. | |
| | p.m. | Called two doors away to borrow envelope from Mrs. A. (non-local) in evening, babysat for Mrs. P. (on the estate and non-local). |
| Monday: | a.m. | Talked over fence to non-local neighbour. |
| | p.m. | |
| Tuesday: | a.m. | |
| | p.m. | In evening rang mother (in East Anglia). |
| Wednesday: | a.m. | 4 non-local housewives called for coffee. |
| | p.m. | Non-local Mrs. K. called to ask her to babysit in evening, babysat for Mrs. K. |
| Thursday: | a.m. | Went to swop magazines with Mrs. P. |
| | p.m. | In evening went to pictures with husband (Mrs. P. babysat). |
| Friday: | a.m. | Mrs. A. went shopping for her. |
| | p.m. | Went to Mrs. K. for afternoon tea. |

Mrs. M. and Mrs. J. bring out the different functions that the estate has for them. In this week Mrs. M. does not think she actually spoke to anyone living on the estate, whereas Mrs. J.'s contacts were almost entirely with neighbours. It also illustrates the relative importance of kin. The number of kin seen by Mrs. M. in a week was not unusual for a local family (remember the account of the Evans christening given in Chapter Five). The diary of Mrs. J. also illustrates the interlocking network of reciprocal obligations on the estate in which she lives. This was true of most non-locals but not of locals.

Willmott and Young wrote that young couples in Woodford

> create, with people of their own age, a group—sometimes small, sometimes large—with functions somewhat similar to these of the East End extended family. It is organized, as the extended family is, by the women, the husbands being drawn into it in a similar sort of way. Its basis is not the kinship tie between mother and daughter but the bond of common interest between wives with young children. The women often treat each other almost as if they were related (1960, p. 106).

Indeed on the estates that I studied they were usually quasi-kin to each other's children. However Willmott and Young's remarks were truer of the non-locals than of the locals, who in many cases could still turn to their extended family.

I am going to pass now to a discussion of the use of gossip in analysing the structure of social relations on the two estates, and this brings out even more strongly the effects of social and geographical mobility. During the initial door-to-door census on both estates it soon became apparent that there was a great deal of gossip and I began to systematically collect as much of it as possible. I noted who said what, about whom and when. Firstly I must add a note about the field situation. Most of the time when I was both formally and informally collecting data there was no one outside the household present. This meant that my informants were free to gossip as much as they wished about other families on the estates. On the other hand they were all aware that I was interviewing all other households on the estate on which they lived and so was in unique possession of a great deal of information about the estate's inhabitants. When I had been in the field for a couple of weeks I began to find that I could gossip with my informants and failed to resist the temptation. The short-term gains were very great because I found that I could swop information and proceed very rapidly. After two such gossip sessions I did not repeat this practice for two reasons that are connected. Firstly there was the purely practical consideration that my informants began to dry up on me when they realized that I may well gossip about them to other people. Secondly there was the ethics of the situation. During these initial stages of the fieldwork I had not developed a satisfactory fieldwork role (see Chapter One). When I realized that the most satisfactory, and the only really honest one was of 'sociological fieldworker' I had to stop gossiping about other households on the estate. In creating this role it was necessary for it to be seen that confidences were kept and that I took no part in gossip. On the larger of the two estates this was adhered to as far as humanly possible, my two major lapses being on the small estate.

In the field I was constantly probed for information by very skilled gossipers and while some information was given away, this was kept to a minimum. My position on both estates was tenuous enough without being caught gossiping. However it was possible to turn this questioning to great advantage in an analysis of the effects of social and geographical mobility on the estates. It became apparent that some people were gossiped about more than others, and I was questioned about them more intensively, whereas other families were virtually unknown and seemed to be socially insignificant. Nobody asked me about them. After my resolve not to gossip as far as possible about estate households with other estate households I not unnaturally found that it was a far slower process in gathering the kind of information in which I was interested. I was no longer prepared to swop gossip and consequently people did not so often gossip with me. I attempted to get round this problem by developing key informants from whom I systematically collected their entire knowledge about other households on the estate. The analysis that follows is based on (*a*) information gathered indirectly whilst interviewing more formally and (*b*) information from the dozen female informants I interviewed specifically about gossip over a period of time.

The analysis of gossip is divided into two parts: (*a*) who gossips about whom and (*b*) the content of this gossip. A careful analysis of who gossips about whom goes a long way towards providing a description of the social structure of the two estates (which can be related to the facts of social and geographical mobility as presented in the earlier chapters of the book). I found this method, although very laborious, more rewarding than the previous methods used, e.g. micro-ecology. I drew up two lists of all the households, one for each estate, and systematically went through all my field material to see who had mentioned them. Theoretically this meant that a household could possibly have been mentioned by all the other households on the estate on which they lived or by no others. Most were towards the latter. Further analysis proved that the households could be divided into groups that could be related to other variables that have already been introduced into this study: stage in family cycle (which is obviously related to age) and to geographical mobility —in terms of whether the households were local or not. At this stage of the analysis, social mobility (defined occupationally and inter-generationally) did not appear as a variable, but it appeared in the second stage of the analysis, that of the content of gossip.

What appeared was that the younger households knew very little of the older households and did not mention them in talking about other households on the estate. It was also the case that the older households did not know the younger households as well as they knew other older households. This was not so well marked, because there were relatively few older households and that as a consequence they did not have as wide a choice of contacts in their own age group on the estate as did the younger households. The younger households on the other hand had no real need to know the older households because they had a wide choice of households in a similar age group.

More significant was the local/non-local distinction. (The age grouping applied to both.) It emerged that the non-locals tended to gossip about other non-locals and similarly that the locals tended to gossip about other locals. Some of the key households, in terms of the number of people that knew them and gossiped about them, were almost unknown across the local/non-local division, i.e. 'gossip cells' as West (1945) called them did not often include both locals and non-locals. For example one informant gave me information about 47 other households, some of which was very detailed. She herself had been geographically mobile and had come to the estate and South Wales three years previously (her husband had a m.q. $= 46 \cdot 2$), but she could only give me information about two local households, one of which was a neighbour. It was unusual for the distinction between locals and non-locals to be as marked as this. A local informant (m.q. $= 31$) gave me information about 24 non-local households out of a total of 34 but did not know anywhere near as much about them. The information was very detailed about the other local households (none of whom she had known before she came to the estate) but much more scanty and often inaccurate about the non-locals.

It was suggested earlier that the estate performed differing functions for the locals and non-locals, the estate providing neighbours for the non-locals whereas the locals were reluctant to be drawn into such reciprocal relationships. The analysis of patterns of gossip would support this. In the groups and cliques that emerged from this analysis there were very few 'cross-cutting alliances' between locals and non-locals and consequently there was very little gossip about locals by non-locals and vice versa.

The fact that the local households gossiped about each other I first thought contradicted my hypothesis that the estate performs differing functions for the locals and non-locals because I did not expect the locals to be able, or want to gossip about other families local or non-local living on the estate. But it really supports this hypothesis, because the local households, although they gossiped with and about the other local households, had developed a different relationship with each other compared with that between the non-local households. One local informant, wife of a teacher (m.q. 38) told me she was very friendly with Mrs. N. and Mrs. O., both locals and she then proceeded to gossip about them to me. She said she was particularly friendly with them because 'they don't want too much from me, we call at arranged times and we are not demanding. That's how it should be.'

It would be wrong to suggest that no local was friendly with a non-local and vice versa, or that there was no gossip about locals among non-locals and vice versa, but there were very few instances of this. The most significant exceptions seemed to be based upon a geographical neighbouring relationship (micro-ecology), i.e. sharing a common garden fence, or on the fact that their children, no respecters of sociological categories, played together.

I now pass to the second part of the analysis of gossip on the two estates: that of its content. On both estates gossip was not only widespread, it was also catholic, there were few aspects of private or public life that were not subject to the examination and scrutiny of other households on the estate. Anyone who has lived in such an environment will know the richness of such gossip, most of which cannot be presented here because not only would it allow individuals to be identified but it would open the author to charges of libel and neighbours to slander. Just two topics of gossip will be concentrated on to give some idea of the richness of gossip as field material, both of which are particularly relevant to the major themes of this book, that of occupation and career mobility, and secondly of kinship information.

Unlike the situation described by Pahl (1965) for a commuter village where other husbands' occupations were often unknown, on both estates the occupations of all husbands seemed to be common knowledge. There was a great interest in the topic among both husbands and wives. It was not sufficient to know what a man's job was, it was necessary to know his actual position. A design engineer who had recently been promoted to being head of a large department when he moved to Swansea was accurately placed in his organization for me by three different informants (all also non-locals). Gossip flowed about applications for a new job by a man in banking; the man himself and his wife never told me about this application but five other households did (again they were all non-locals). This interest in career pattern was almost universal and as pointed out in Chapter One led me to stress the centrality of the career in the middle class life style.

Groups of husbands from the estate, when out at a pub together would talk about their jobs and try to compare their relative positions in their respective hierarchies. Very detailed information about their positions would be discussed over a pint at Sunday lunch time and later this would be passed to their wives. It then entered the estate gossip network. Because all the husbands in this case were non-locals (as were their wives) and the friends of their wives were similarly non-local, this information never passed to the locals.

Closely related to gossip about careers was that about social mobility. I have no evidence of social mobility as opposed to geographical mobility having any effect on the structure of social relations on the estate. This is a major conclusion of this research and is the reverse of the conclusions stated in Chapter Four of the book about the effects of social and geographical mobility on the family. The facts of social mobility were a subject for gossip but their effects on groups and cliques or participation on the estate were negligible. Of the 31 households that had been socially mobile (as earlier defined), I was told about 25 of these by people outside the households concerned. This gives some indication of the nature and detail of the gossip on both estates. The facts of social mobility were not hidden. A fact which is relevant to the second area of gossip to be considered, that of kinship.

Kinship information circulated in the gossip networks of both estates. There was as much interest in it as there was in occupation and career. Just as details of occupational position allowed other households to be 'placed', particularly in relation to oneself, so kinship information was similarly seized upon. For example living on one of the estates were the in-laws of a very famous (local) sportsman; this fact was repeated to me by many of the other families living on the estate. All the local households knew about them but not all of the non-locals. Similarly any kin connection that could be used to link a family living on the estate with a famous product was known, e.g. 'his father is Bloggs fish-paste'. Siblings of people living on the estate that were in some way notable were often brought up in general gossip. When I asked about a household, from a housewife who lived two doors away, after I was told the husband's job, I was told about his brother-in-law (a well-known author) of whom it was expected that I would have heard. But this kind of kinship information was often limited to gossip cells that only contained locals or only non-locals.

Across this division there was little gossip about kin and although there was gossip about occupation it was of a different kind. Instead of the detail about actual position within a hierarchy the gossip was far more in terms of national or universal occupational stereotypes. There was a local estate agent living on one of the estates and another local household told me in detail about the development of his business, how he had made his money, what his father and mother did, and what his wife's father did. The non-locals were not in possession of this kind of information and that which I was told was often highly inaccurate and inflammatory, relating to stereotypes of estate agents being 'sharks' and extremely shrewd dealers. Similarly there was a non-local senior academic about whose entire and bewildering career I was told in great detail by other informants, all non-local. Before I interviewed him I was in possession of an accurate biography picked up from the gossip network of other non-locals. To the locals he was, however, an 'absent minded professor' because of his (not very) eccentric appearance and unusual gardening techniques. (Compare the situation discussed by Gluckman where a character in a Jane Austen novel never actually appears in the book 'yet in the gossip of others we see him as an individual, influencing their dealings with one another' (1963, p. 309).)

## 3 Conclusions and Summary

Firstly, there is the methodological point that gossip, in terms of who gossips about whom and with whom, is of great value in the analysis of the social structure of the estates. Epstein wrote about a very different context:

> . . . victims of gossip are rarely seized upon at random . . . to be talked about in one's absence, in however derogatory terms, is to be conceded a measure of social importance in the gossip set; not to be talked about is the mark of social insignificance, of exclusion from the set. In other words, gossip denotes a certain community of interest, even if the limits of the community can only be vaguely defined (1961, pp. 58-9).

On both estates there are two gossip sets, each containing several gossip cells. Rarely do these cells, or the sets as a whole, contain both locals *and* non-locals.

Secondly these two sets can be directly related to the facts of geographical mobility, but not to social mobility as usually defined. So perhaps in future any operational definition of social mobility should include some notion of geographical mobility.

Thirdly the content of the gossip re-emphasized the importance of the career to the middle class life style and that although kinship information is still used to place people even among the geographically mobile, national occupation stereotypes are becoming more usual. Loudon has made a similar point: 'where an individual has no extensive local network of kin ties, evaluation of unusual behaviour is often in terms of general or "national" norms of expectation regarding the performance for example of occupation of "social class" role' (1961, p. 349).

Finally I would like to consider some more general points about gossip, in particular those raised by Gluckman in his stimulating treatment of the topic. He concludes his article with what he calls 'the rules of gossipship', which he begins by writing 'the important things about gossip and scandal are that generally these are enjoyed by people about others with whom they are in close relationship' (1963, p. 313). On both estates an examination of gossip shows that those who have been geographically mobile are more likely to be in close relationship with each other than with the locals who have not been geographically mobile. Similarly the locals gossip about each other far more than they do about the non-locals. Gluckman continues that 'the right to gossip about certain people is a privilege which is only extended to a person when he or she is accepted as a member of this group or set. It is the hall-mark of membership. Hence rights to gossip serve to mark off a particular group from other groups.' On the two estates it was not just this right to gossip that marked off groups but also the content of their gossip. Gluckman writes that 'when you gossip about your friends to other mutual friends you are demonstrating that you all belong to one set'. On the estates this was the case, and in the next chapter I analyse one incident that helped to widen the division between locals and non-locals, between those who had experienced geographical mobility and those who had not.

# CHAPTER SEVEN

# An Analysis of an Event

## 1 *Introduction*

In any given social situation individuals are faced with the possibility of alternative modes of action. Any analysis of a social situation should be concerned with the way individuals and groups are able to exercise choices within the limits of a specified social structure. A prerequisite, then, should be some outline of the social structure within which action takes place. In practice this is not always possible.

When I began interviewing on the two new privately owned middle class housing estates the situation seemed at first very close to that described by Marx in *The Eighteenth Brumaire of Louis Napoleon*, when he referred to the French peasantry as being 'formed by the simple addition of equal magnitudes, much as potatoes in a sack form a sack of potatoes'. The mid-twentieth century spiralist may not bear immediate resemblance to the mid-nineteenth century French peasantry but the above quotation suggests some of the initial difficulties with which I felt I was faced when attempting to analyse the social structure of a new housing development. There is, however, an approach utilized by anthropologists working in Africa that offers a solution. (Gluckman: 1940, 1942, 1958 and Mitchell: 1956.) This chapter is an attempt to apply their techniques in an urban situation in Britain, and focuses on a 'dramatic occurrence'. It takes the form of a case history of a specific incident, or series of incidents associated with the signing of a petition on the larger of the two estates studied.

## 2  *The Public Events*

The public side of the issues and events described below can be briefly summarized by an account of the public enquiry held before a change in the town's development plan could be made to provide for the erection of multi-storey halls of residence for the local university after the purchase of a site adjacent to the estate.

The case for the changes was based on three main points: the national need for university expansion, its local importance, and the preservation of this site from speculative housing development. The local Ratepayers' Association had officially come round to support the university and as counsel for the university said, 'It is not often that objectors become supporters in an enquiry of this kind.' Later it is possible to suggest how this came about, at least on the housing development adjacent to the proposed university site.

A crucial factor for the local residents was the actual number of students that would live in the new residences. 1400 was quoted at the public enquiry by the university. This figure is important because it was manipulated widely by different individuals and groups on the housing development at different times.

The local residents had been adamant against the development but had become supporters of the university: or so runs the account in the local press. In fact this was not so. They had been persuaded that the real choice was between the proposed university development and speculative housing, and not between development and no development, consequently they became reluctant supporters of the university. There had emerged among the residents a compromise position of wanting 'reasonable assurances' on three main points: on the maintenance of the natural beauty of the area, restrictions of the height of the new buildings and most strongly on the amount of traffic through the housing development. On all three points assurances were received. The spokesman for the housing development said 'we have no objections, in fact, we would welcome pedestrian access from the university site across the estate. But we object to heavy vehicles.' In conclusion the local residents were given the assurance that 'the least possible interference with the estate will take place'.

Permission was granted for a change to be made in the town's development plan.

## 3   *Dissenters, Hedgers and Ditchers, Activists*

Having briefly described the public events, attention will now be concentrated on events concerning the 89 households living on the estate. They are divided between those who signed the petition and those who did not, or dissented from doing so. Those who did not sign have been called *dissenters*. Those who signed the petition have been further divided into two groups: *hedgers* and *ditchers*. The former adopted the compromise position, with 'adequate assurances' they were supporters of the university. The ditchers continued to object and would admit no compromise. Within this inclusive classification are a small group; the *activists*: those who took round the petition. Ideologically all the activists were hedgers.

The petition was taken round by the activists on a Friday evening and the following weekend. Of the 89 households, two were away that weekend and one was overlooked by mistake. So 86 households were asked to sign: 51 did so and 35 dissented. (All the household signed or did not sign, there was no 'mixed' household. Although husbands and wives often disagreed in their emphasis about whether to sign the petition or not, it is possible to use households as units.)

For any argument based on participation of individuals in this event it is necessary to at least attempt to control for two independent variables. Firstly willingness to sign petitions at all. It was possible that some refused to sign 'on principle': all the dissenters denied this when asked but there is some further evidence which is also related to the second variable: whether dissenters did not sign because of antipathy towards the activists. Before this issue of the university development, two of the activists petitioned against a road closure. Not as many households were approached to sign: 74. All but two signed, both maintained that the closure should take place, but both signed the second petition. So there was no feeling against signing petitions 'on principle'. It is not possible to control for the fact that a third activist also took round the second petition but from a knowledge of the field it is possible to say that nobody refused to sign because of him.

The petition form was headed by the legend of the local Ratepayers' Association and stated that the university had bought the site and was seeking planning permission to build multi-storey accommodation for up to 3,000 students of both sexes: 'And we the undersigned would like to protest against the wholesale destruction of amenities of the . . . estate and to object to the danger and inconvenience that the resulting increase in traffic would cause.' In the situation of latent if not manifest neighbourliness (Mann 1954) and of quasi-kin groups and in the face of activists whose belief in the rightness of their cause was Cromwellian, dissent was not to be expected. So it is very surprising that 35 households did in fact dissent in this situation.

It is necessary here to suggest the significance of the petition. It brought out into the open conflicts which are normally not apparent. It illustrates the relationships between the two groups with different reference groups and career orientation; between those whose careers will take them beyond the town and for whom the estate and the town are only relatively brief stopping places, and those who expect their careers to take place within the local community. Between those Watson called 'spiralists' and those he called 'burgesses' or what Merton had earlier called 'cosmopolitans' and 'locals'.[1] Between those who have been geographically mobile and those who have not.

This can be made clearer if the basic differences between the dissenters and the hedgers and ditchers are outlined. Only 13 of the 35 dissenting households had members who had been born or brought up within 15 miles of the town compared with 37 of the 51 hedgers and ditchers. More importantly 33 of the dissenting households expected their future careers to take them away from the town, compared with 11 out of 51 of the hedgers and ditchers (and three of these had close neighbouring relations with the activists). Another 18 of the hedgers and ditchers

[1] There is a danger in too glib a use of these hyphenated neologisms, opposite sides of the equation are not necessarily transferable from neologism to neologism. Spiralists are not necessarily cosmopolitan as Merton wished to use the term and Merton's term local may not be applicable to all burgesses.

thought that they would move from the development within five years, but stay in the town either with increased prosperity or to make adjustments with a stage change in the life cycle. This included all the activists.

Of the 35 dissenting households 29 had a member that had been to a university compared with only five out of the 51 signers of the petition. Another correlation with signing the petition is with professed voting behaviour. Of the 34 non-Conservative voting households on the housing development 29 did not sign the petition, i.e. five non-Conservative voters signed the petition: two Liberal and three Labour (one of whom was a neighbour of an activist).[1]

As a further indication of differences between dissenters and hedgers and ditchers: no dissenting household took the morning daily local paper, 17 hedgers and ditchers did, and less than a quarter of the dissenters took the evening daily local paper (seven households) compared with three-quarters (38 households) of the hedgers and ditchers. All households had been asked their opinions about the introduction of comprehensive schools. The results are tabulated below.

|  | *For* | *Against* | *Don't know* | *Totals* |
|---|---|---|---|---|
| Dissenters | 21 | 6 | 8 | 35 |
| Hedgers and ditchers | 19 | 20 | 12 | 51 |
| Total | 40 | 26 | 20 | 86 |

It can be seen that more signers of the petition were against the introduction of comprehensive schools than were for, whereas the dissenters were 3 : 1 in favour. Too much importance must not be given to these details of professed voting behaviour, opinions on comprehensive schools and local newspaper consumption but they are indicators of broad differences in

[1] Ratepayers' Associations are sometimes seen as a Conservative Party 'front' organization, although in this particular ward at the last local election, Conservative, Labour and Ratepayers fought the ward and the Conservatives gained it from the Ratepayers. But from the interviews it can safely be said that nobody objected to the petition on the party political grounds that it was under the legend of the Local Ratepayers.

orientation, and interest in the local community (Larsen and Edelstein: 1961) of the two groups.

Merton described the locals in Rovere as 'parochial' and pre-occupied with local problems to the virtual exclusion of the national and international scene; and cosmopolitans as identifying and relating themselves to issues and events and social organizations outside the local community. Taking university expansion as an issue, the hedgers and ditchers did not think of the university as part of the local scene but as part of wider affairs. This can be shown by a content analysis of the arguments used about the university development. The dissenters tended to stress the national importance of universities and that the university was a great, some said the only asset to the community. But the ditchers in particular stressed the nuisance value of students, the destruction of local rural amenities by the proposed development by invading hordes, the decline in the value of their houses and the shattering of their peace and quiet. Their arguments were what Tucker (1966) has recently called the '*Lebensraum* Fear': 'given the slightest opportunity innumerable predators will swoop down and swallow up all the tidy, respectable underpopulated private estates.' (Similarly Collison: 1963.) The local/cosmopolitan dimension refers to the scale of the social environment in which the individual sees himself, and the hedgers and ditchers were not prepared to include the university within their environment. Also for the dissenters, universities were part of their experience, for the hedgers and ditchers they were not.

During the initial stages of the observation of these events it was thought that the non-locals would be against the university development because of their transience and lack of ties with a locality that reputedly takes great pride in its educational institutions. Similarly I thought that the locals would support it for precisely these reasons, together with the fact that the university is one of the largest employers in the town and that as locals they would realize its economic significance. This proved not to be so. The locals although orientated towards the community economically and often in terms of their social relations and future careers tended to oppose the university development. This was particularly evident among the ditchers whose interpretation of their interest was very 'parochial' indeed, to use

Merton's term. It was the cosmopolitans that welcomed the university development, people who had few ties with the community and who would move on.

The dissenters have been more mobile, have lived in a succession of communities in different parts of the country and differ markedly in their attachment to the town and in attitudes towards leaving it, compared with the hedgers and ditchers. Like Merton's locals and cosmopolitans the hedgers and ditchers and the dissenters did not differ significantly in age or family composition. But unlike the locals and cosmopolitans in Rovere they did differ in education and occupation suggesting that their differing orientation towards the community may be a reflection of educational and occupational differences which was associated with greater geographical and social mobility for the dissenters.

Here I will describe a typical dissenter and a typical signer of the petition. In these descriptions will be recognized the characteristics of the mobile and immobile with which I have been concerned in this book.

Mrs. C. was 34 with two children and dissented from signing the petition. (Her husband has a m.q. of 46.) Both she and her husband have been socially mobile, and both went to a provincial university. She has a music degree and her husband a science degree from the same university. He is a Ph.D and now is an engineer at a large metallurgical plant. She taught in a primary school before the birth of her first child. Since marriage they have lived in two towns in the Midlands, in suburban London, South Wales and expect to move to Scotland within a year. They have no local kin. At the public meeting of the local Ratepayers she was quite prepared to speak out in favour of the university, in marked contrast to the hedging and ditching wives who remained silent. She argued that it was better the university had the land than a speculative housing developer, but more strongly that the university must expand and that it was a good thing for the country that they should. All her friends on the estate dissented and three of the four came from households that had members that had been to a university. All four were non-locals. She belonged to the Labour Party and two associations that were nationwide.

Throughout these events the ditchers were the most difficult respondents. Their opposition to the university unfortunately manifested itself in opposition to the fieldworker as a visible and accessible representative of the university.

Mr. D. a ditcher, aged 40, married with no children, left school at 16. He and his wife have always lived in the town (m.q. = 28). He has always worked in the 'motor trade' and now owns a garage. He does not expect to live on the estate for ever, but will not leave the town. He does not have any friends, 'not what I would call friends', on the estate. He is a regular member of a chapel and the local Chamber of Trade. He said of the university development, 'I don't want them here, I bought this house and now they are going to ruin my privacy. Why can't they go somewhere else? We pay enough in rates not to have to put up with this sort of thing.' He was surprised that some people had not signed the petition: 'I thought they were all sensible people.' He has a very localized kin network, seeing both his and his wife's siblings regularly.

Ditchers were not activists. The activists were two households, neighbours. They were born and brought up well away from the town (m.q.s of 46·5 and 44). Both had been socially and geographically mobile. Neither household contained a member that had been to a university. Both thought that it was unlikely that they would move from the town, both husbands being in their early 40's, but both expected to be in a financial position to move from the estate within five years. For both the activist households the petition itself was at least as important as the issues involved. They varied the number of students with the likelihood of people signing the petition (the petition itself quotes more than double the correct figure, a fact of which the activists were aware), the number being increased with resistance to signing. Several dissenters claimed that while the activists were on the doorstep the supposed upheaval accompanying the university expansion became steadily more exaggerated the longer they refused to sign.

When it was clear that the choice was not between development and no development but between speculative housing development and university development, the local Ratepayers advised against a further petition. But against this advice the activists took round the petition described above.

Why were the activists so active? This is an example of *cross-*

*mobility* (Plowman, Minchinton and Stacey: 1962) but in the opposite direction to its original usage when it was used to describe leaving the local, and by implication traditional, social system for a non-tradition, and by implication non-local, social system involving important changes in attitudes without necessarily altering the level of status. The petition for the activists was one of the mechanisms by which they were attempting to enter a local, if not a traditional social system. An examination of their associational membership pattern supports this argument. Both households were members of very local and very traditional associations important in local culture. Both were active in politics at the ward level. One household had been in the town two years, the other three. One activist, after the report of the public enquiry had been published in the local press made a very revealing remark when he saw that he was mentioned by name: 'that should do me a bit of good.' He appeared to be more pleased about this than in getting 'adequate assurances' from the university.

Having a neighbouring relationship with an activist was an important factor in signing the petition (i.e. micro-ecology). None of the 35 dissenting households were neighbours of the activists, neither in the geographical sense (the closest dissenter lived seven doors away) nor in the definitional sense of being able to call without warning. There were three households who by other characteristics alone may have been expected to dissent but were neighbours of the activists. To the fieldworker they stressed they had no objection to the university itself but did not want heavy traffic through the estate. They included a household who said they did not sign when in fact they did.

## 4  *The Consequences for Social Relationships*

The earlier quotation from Marx indicates some of the confusion felt during the initial observation when the fieldworker was faced with a bewilderingly tangled network of friendship ties, neighbouring ties, quasi-kin groups, ties of common geographical origin, of occupation, of common school or university. On this housing development it was possible to identify over fifty groupings varying from groups with a recognizable structure, through quasi-groups to almost casual meetings (Mayer 1966), some permanent, some ephemeral. The list was not of course exhaustive and was constantly becoming longer. But very few of these groupings cross the local/non-local division, and as there is a close correspondence, the hedger and ditcher/dissenter division. Those that do, are based mainly on micro-ecology: the fact of geographical neighbouring. Two of these groupings will be described to show the consequences of the events described above.

Firstly there was a group of six men who went drinking together every Sunday lunch time. There were four locals and two non-locals. Two of the locals had been to school with each other and had renewed their friendship when they discovered each other on the same housing development. The third was a cousin of the first (father's, sister's son) and the fourth was a colleague of the second. The two non-locals were neighbours of the second and third locals. But the two non-locals had very little contact with the others besides Sunday drinking; neither their wives nor their children being particularly friendly. All four locals signed the petition: the two non-locals dissented. The locals took up the hedging position of wanting 'adequate assurances', rather than the ditching position of absolute opposition. On the weekend of the petition they went drinking as usual and the petition was the main topic of conversation. They told each other whether they had signed or not, the locals were very surprised that the two non-locals had not signed and they argued vigorously. Both non-locals defended their dissent strongly and called the locals 'narrow-minded' and they appealed to the wider issues of university expansion. The following Sunday one non-local was unwell and the other was away. The four locals went drinking as usual. They decided that on future Sundays they would go to a different pub because it would be less crowded and that the beer would be better. It would involve driving, the first pub was within walking distance which was its original attraction. The two non-locals were told of the change of plans indirectly through their wives. Both independently decided that they would not go to the second pub because it was too far and they did not want to drive. Two Sundays later they stopped going to the original pub because they had both started to go to a third pub on a weekday evening with two other men from the housing estate, both also non-locals. One was a colleague, the other met through the friendship of their children. When the two original non-locals were asked about this change and why they did not go with the original four locals any more on Sundays, neither mentioned the hiatus that had occurred in their attendance immediately after the petition but both mentioned the petition itself. And then said how much more they had in common with the two others they now drank with during the week.

The second group was a weekday coffee morning based on six wives who were hosts in rotation. The other five attending the sixth, together with any others that that week's hostess had invited. There were four non-locals and two locals but all had dissented. They had discussed the petition in advance and had said that they would not sign it because they thought it would be a good thing if the university developed the land. The group consisted of four wives who lived in close proximity and between whom there was intense neighbouring relationships: three non-locals plus one local; together with two others from a distance, one of whose sons was very friendly with the daughter of one of the other four, and her neighbour, a local. On the Wednesday after the petition they met as usual but before they arrived one of the activist wives called to discuss arrangements about the 'daily woman' they shared. They had no other contact. She was asked to stay to coffee, which she did, but had not realized it was *the* coffee morning. The activist wife said she felt awful when she saw 'the opposition trooping down the drive'. She left as soon as she could and until she did the atmosphere was very strained. When she left the hostess quickly told the others she had not really invited her, she was only being polite. As soon as she had gone they gossiped about her and the petition. Here face-to-face contact had if anything reinforced the division between the dissenters and the rest, gossip being confined to those who did not differ on the issues at stake.

## 5   Conclusions

In discussing 'The Neighbourhood Idea' Dennis, echoing Marx, has written 'people seem to find it extraordinarily difficult to realize that mere living together in the same locality can result in a conglomeration of very little sociological importance. The difficulty is immeasurably increased when the people in the locality are sociologically homogeneous' (1958, p. 191). But as Frankenberg has recently stressed 'however large scale the society we wish to study and however massive the residential unit there is always social interaction in small face-to-face groups' (1966a, p. 149) (see also Pons, 1961, who shows the value of intensive small group studies in shedding light on the system of social relations in an urban situation, in this case Stanleyville in the Congo). By close and detailed observation of this face to face interaction it is possible to describe social processes.

If the fieldworker is fortunate there will be some social drama that will perhaps reveal some underlying conflict of interests. The nature of a middle class private housing estate makes it very difficult to find situations in which conflicts became socially manifest.

The petition provided an opportunity for such an analysis but has the obvious weakness that it was not an observable incident in the usual anthropological sense. Compared for example with Gluckman's description of a ceremony whereby a new bridge in Zululand is opened. He isolated the important elements in the ceremony and then traces each of these elements back into the larger society, to demonstrate their significance in the ceremony he has described. Or compared with what is perhaps the finest example of event analysis: Mitchell's analysis of the Kalela Dance, where by working outwards from the specific social situation of the Dance the whole social fabric of the Copper Belt is taken in. It is only when this process has been followed to a conclusion that he returns to the dance and explains its significance.

The housing estate never acted as an entity and only rarely did any happening involve more than a relatively few households. But the petition was at least presented to most households and this crucial occasion revealed and articulated the division between locals and non-locals. It was not as circumscribed an event as the funeral described by Loudon, nor as temporarily limited as the bridge opening described by Gluckman, nor as dramatic even as the Kalela Dance described by Mitchell but it allowed in Turner's penetrating phrase 'a limited area of transparency on the otherwise opaque surface of regular, uneventful social life' (1957, p. 93), through which the relationships between spiralists and burgesses could be observed.

# CHAPTER EIGHT

# Towards a Theory of Social Mobility

This final chapter is divided into two parts, (i) what has been learned, i.e. the conclusions of the research. This will in part be a repetition of conclusions that appear in earlier chapters and (ii) what it means, i.e. the theoretical significance of my conclusions.

The major conclusion is that Watson's distinction between 'spiralists' and 'burgesses' is empirically verifiable and theoretically valuable; however, as I shall argue below, it has limitations. These two groups within the middle class are identifiable not only by their differing mobility experience, both social and geographical (what I called their differing mobility 'context'), but also by their differing relationship with their kin, and also by their relationship with each other.

Chapters Two and Three of the book were designed to give a quantitative backing to Watson's analysis and Chapters Four to Seven were designed to show the effects of the differing contexts of mobility both on the styles of life and on the structure of social relations of the 120 families studied. The detailed conclusions on the family are given at the end of Chapter Four: their importance may be emphasized by a comparison with those of Willmott and Young in Woodford. They ask at the end of their statistical appendix,

> 'what conclusions can be drawn from the complex series of tables in this appendix? Social mobility, it seems, does affect people's contacts with their parents in the following ways:
> 1. Contacts with fathers are affected rather than with mothers.

2. Sons' contacts with fathers are affected rather than daughters'.

But we would like to add a vital qualification: the statistical evidence for these conclusions is slight, and before any generalizations can be safely made on the relationship between occupational mobility and even the limited aspect of family structure we are considering, a great deal of further research needs to be done' (1960, p. 167).

Amongst the families that I studied who had not been socially mobile, i.e. who came from a middle class background, the father-in-law/father-son/son-in-law link was structurally very important. It was in fact the link through which aid flowed between the units in the extended family. Geographical mobility obviously affected the amount of contact between members of the extended family, i.e. the locals saw more of their kin than the non-locals. However, in terms of the functioning of the extended family it was social mobility, as usually defined and not geographical mobility that was the important variable. Amongst the socially immobile families, regardless of whether they had been geographically mobile or not, the male part of the extended family was important. As all the families studied who had been socially mobile had also been geographically mobile there was a low contact rate amongst the members of these extended families. Because the families from a working class background could not be in receipt of the same kind of aid as those from middle class backgrounds, there was not a corresponding increase in emphasis on the male part of the extended family structure that I have been able to demonstrate for the entirely middle class extended family.

The effect of social (occupational) mobility and of geographical mobility on the structure of social relationships differed in the neighbourhood compared to their effect on the extended family. In the neighbourhood (in this case the two estates studied) an analysis of the structure of social relationships through gossip and event analysis showed that geographical mobility had more influence than social (occupational) mobility. The major division being between the locals and the non-locals. Social (occupational) mobility was unimportant on both estates in the structuring of social relationships, except in as far as it was associated with geographical mobility.

To summarize, there are contrasting effects of social (occupational) mobility and geographical mobility on (1) the family and (2) the neighbourhood. On the family it was social (occupational) mobility and not geographical mobility that had the stronger effect on the structure of social relationships, whereas on the neighbourhood it was geographical mobility and not social (occupational) mobility that had the stronger effect.

Willmott and Young's remarks quoted above also raise the methodological point about how family structure is to be measured. They write of 'statistical evidence' but I would follow Rosser and Harris's strictures against any apparently precise measure of family structure. The quantitative evidence that I have produced about contact between and geographical distribution of members of the extended family can only be used to show that the male part of the middle class extended family structure is at least as important as the more usually stressed mother–daughter link. The evidence that I would want to base my arguments most strongly upon, however, is not the quantitative but the qualitative evidence about aid between members of the extended family.

This leads to the methodological conclusions, which in their implications are probably more important for future research than are my substantive findings. Although it may have been possible to identify both spiralists and burgesses from a more statistical study it would not have been possible to study the relationships between these two groups. The major point being that it is both possible and valuable to use the intensive techniques of the social anthropologist in what at first sight was not a very promising environment. From the evidence that I gained by these methods I can argue far more strongly about aspects of family structure than I would have been able to do from the more statistical approach that has hitherto been used. Neither of the two estates studied were in any way a sample in the technical sense of the word, both were treated as complete universes and I hope that I have shown that the gains were greater than the possible losses through their unrepresentativeness. Obviously other investigators have studied individual families in greater depth, e.g. Bott, but she did not study the neighbours of her families as well. One of the great weaknesses in studies of social networks or sets is that they tend to be so ego-orientated and the investigator relies upon ego's word for what goes on elsewhere in the network. There is little attempt to go down the network as it were. On the two estates studied, however, it was possible to look at one aspect of ego's set completely: to examine the total network of neighbouring. (Chapter Six shows how this network can be related to mobility.) One of the great weaknesses of the genealogies I collected was that in most cases it was impossible to go very far into the genealogy interviewing other members of the kin network.

Having established the network of social relations for the two estates I was extraordinarily fortunate to have an event that encompassed the whole of one estate. As Gluckman has written, by situational analysis it should be possible to use the actions of individuals and groups within these situations to exhibit the morphology of the social structure (1960, p. 8). This was my aim in Chapter Seven, which I see as the culmination of my analysis of mobility and the justification of my methodology. Gluckman wrote in the same paper that, 'if we are going to penetrate more deeply into the actual process by which persons and groups live together within a social system, under a culture, we have to employ a series of connected cases occurring within the same area of social life' (1960, p.10). I hope that in this study of middle-class families I have been able to show by this method how they 'live together within a social system'.

Social mobility as usually studied, to reiterate some of my criticisms that are in Chapter Three, depends upon a large sample. The work of D. V. Glass *et al.* usually serves as a model. Aaronovitch has parodied this methodology, but unfortunately he is not far from the truth when he writes, 'Ask people how they grade occupations in terms of status and from that compile a table which allocates the population according to the view they hold themselves collectively. Divide the table into upper, middle and lower and then study the transitions from one status to another. Describe the result as the degree of social mobility' (1961, p. 116). If one wishes to be polite one can regret the present concentration on computing rates of (occupational) mobility, or one can be rude and call it mindless head counting. It is certainly all too easy to end up with results the implications of which are impossible to grasp. An example of this is the Index of Association computed by Glass and his associates. It is as if I put the same emphasis on my 'mobility quotient', which I most certainly do not. The end results of so many studies of social mobility seem to be the equivalent of my Table 2:1 which I see as a starting point of the analysis proper. (The first step beyond the Glass type of study, that of numerous international comparisons, has already been made. The second step is considerably rarer, that of comparisons over time, although there is the recent contribution of Thernstrom, which is significantly based on a community study.)

The sub-divisions of Glass's occupation index are neither classes nor functional groups. By his methods it would have been impossible to identify spiralists and burgesses, groups which I have shown do have an empirical reality and are not just the product of the sociological imagination. To make this occupational index more realistic it is necessary to add at least one more variable, this work has been concerned with the addition of this variable, that of geographical mobility. If this variable is considered, as well as that of occupational mobility, it is possible to divide occupational hierarchies into two groups: locals and non-locals. The relationship between these two groups was the subject of Chapters Six and Seven. Social mobility has hitherto always been measured in the mass and yet it is the individuals who do the moving. By a close examination of the movers as individuals, or in this case as individual households, it was possible to show the importance of geographical mobility as a variable in mobility studies.

Miller's trend report on social mobility, which is perhaps the most valuable document on the subject (run close by Sorokin's early work), stresses that 'the resort to concentration on occupational prestige as *the* indicator of mobility is a choice largely based on the relative simplicity of the procedures involved' (1960, p. 4) and continues that 'on the grounds of economy if not always of sensitivity it (occupational prestige) likely merits its premier place in the study of social mobility. The danger lies in believing that occupational prestige has the only place' (p. 5). Quite so, it is at least necessary to make some theoretical provision for geographical mobility. Miller concludes his report by arguing that the expansion of the focus of mobility studies will require utilizing qualitative materials as well as quantitative and suggests that hitherto there has been too strong an emphasis on quantitative data. Miller concludes,

> Unfortunately many of our most sophisticated discussions of occupational mobility (and we have some very fine ones) tend to have little reference to the wider context in which occupational mobility takes place. The first step may be the digging of brute facts; the second step which has not been adequately done in any nation is to put the findings in historical and sociological contexts (p. 60).

The digging of brute facts of mobility as Miller calls it, has exacted a great deal of sociological effort, and has often been inadequate because, as I have already stressed, there is a marked tendency to ignore geographical mobility as a variable. In the case of this book the brute facts were presented in Chapters Two and Three. I then attempted to put them in their sociological context, at any rate of the family and the neighbourhood. As Miller pointed out this is not usually done.

Miller wrote that 'the study of social mobility is a study of change, of movement. It is no easy matter to set it off precisely from other types of change which sociologists investigate, e.g. geographical mobility, job-shifting, for at many points these various mobility phenomena intersect' (1960, p. 1). However, I want to argue that, in terms of the interpersonal relations of the families studied, it is neither very helpful nor very meaningful to set social mobility off precisely from geographical mobility. They are so intimately intertwined that any valid theory of 'social mobility' must include notions of both geographical mobility and of what is now called social mobility, i.e. occupational mobility.

An example of an advance in mobility studies beyond that of computing rates of occupational mobility is the paper by Blau, 'Social Mobility and Interpersonal Relations' (1956) in which he correlates types of mobility with other variables. I will argue below that because he ignores geographical mobility his analysis does not have the depth that it might have acquired.

Blau postulates a four-way division of any population based (*a*) upon a division of the occupational hierarchy into 'highs' and 'lows' and (*b*) two groups who have experienced mobility;

the result being that the population is divided into:

    stationary highs
    stationary lows
    upwardly mobile
    downwardly mobile.

He then presents empirical evidence 'on the ways of acting and thinking of people in these four categories which reveal several distinct patterns' (1956, p. 291), His paper is well enough known for it not to be reiterated in detail. Briefly he reminds us that there are correlations between these four categories and family size, voting behaviour, tendency to join trade unions, prejudice and feelings of security.

Just as I criticize both Glass and Blau for not including geographical mobility in their analyses of social mobility I must similarly point out that Watson tended to ignore intergenerational social (occupational) mobility. For although I have argued that geographical mobility is often the key factor in the structuring of social relations it must still be used in conjunction with more traditional notions of social mobility. In the neighbourhood, on the estates, Watson's distinction between spiralists and burgesses was crucial but also it must be remembered that spiralists from a working class background had a different family structure compared with these from a middle class background. The utility of the occupational mobility studies of Glass *et al.* and the radical departure from this tradition by Watson are both weakened by their underemphasis of one part of a wider notion of a truly 'social' mobility that includes both occupation and geographical mobility.

I would like to extend their analyses and postulate a similar model to that of Blau described above but different in one vital respect, I want to add the variable of geographical mobility. This will produce a theoretical division of any population that is considerably more complicated than that of Blau but I would argue that it is more realistic. Also I am going to change the terminology slightly in one important respect, instead of 'highs' and 'lows' I will use middle and working class (non-manual and manual occupations, ignoring the problems of an 'upper' class). The resulting model is shown in Table 8:1.

To fill all eight boxes in this theoretical table would require

# TABLE: 8:1.
# Mobility

| | | GEOGRAPHICALLY | |
|---|---|---|---|
| | | MOBILE | IMMOBILE |
| SOCIALLY MOBILE | MIDDLE CLASS | 1 ↘ | 3 ↓ |
| | WORKING CLASS | 2 ↗ | 4 ↑ |
| SOCIALLY IMMOBILE | MIDDLE CLASS | 5 → | 7 ○ |
| | WORKING CLASS | 6 → | 8 ○ |

1   Downwardly socially mobile and geographically mobile
2   Upwardly socially mobile   "    "    "
3   Downwardly socially mobile and geographically immobile
4   Upwardly socially mobile and   "    "
5   Socially immobile and geographically mobile
6   "  "  "  "  "
7   Immobile, both socially and geographically
8   "   "  "  "  "

a considerable sample, e.g. a Banbury. The evidence from community studies suggests, however, that this is not an unrealistic division of a population. Young and Willmott, in the first half of *Family and Kinship in East London* are concerned with box number eight, and in the second half of the book, the part on Greenleigh, they are concerned with box number six. Throughout their book there are references to people who would be in box number two.

The subject-matter of this work is similarly limited to only part of the model, but it does present in detail the importance of geographical mobility as a variable. In this study of 120 middle class families there was no downward social mobility by the definitions used. The families, in fact, would fall into the following boxes:

Number two:   those who started from a working class home and had been geographically as well as socially mobile.

Number five:   those who came from a middle class home and had been geographically mobile in the course of the husband's career.

Number seven: those who came from a middle class home and had stayed in the town in which they were brought up, i.e. the locals or burgesses.

It was theoretically possible, indeed I hoped to have representatives of box number four, those who had come from a working class background and had stayed in the same town, but unfortunately there were none living on either estate studied. It is likely that from the point of view of the present research these would have been most interesting sociologically.

If I had retained Blau's classifications, the families that I studied would all have been either 'stationary highs' or 'upwardly mobile'. There would have been no way of distinguishing between those who had been geographically mobile and those who had not. The fieldwork showed that the major difference was between the locals, those who had not been geographically mobile (and it so happened they had not been socially mobile either) and the non-locals who had been geographically mobile (some had been socially mobile and some had not). Blau's paper was called 'Social Mobility and *Interpersonal Relations*' (my emphasis) but from my research I would argue that in the study of interpersonal relations geographical mobility must be considered together with social mobility as he defined it.

It has become a sociological commonplace that the mobile man is a 'marginal man', 'poised on the edge of several groups but not fully accepted by any of them', as Merton wrote (1957 p. 265). Lipset and Bendix similarly argue that 'The mobile individual, who is in many ways a marginal man, retaining old ties and experiences, is more likely to be subjected to cross pressure than the non-mobile person' (1959, p. 69). Blau stresses that (mobile persons) 'are marginal men, in some respects out of tune with others both in their new and original strata in the occupational hierarchy', and so he postulates as his central hypothesis that, 'the dilemmas faced by mobile individuals in their interpersonal relations inhibit social integration and are responsible for many aspects of their attitude and conduct' (1956, p. 290).

None of my data will support this hypothesis. The key fact against it was surely the ability of the geographically mobile to be socially integrated with each other. It will be remembered that the geographically mobile came both from the working class and the middle class, so some had been intergenerationally mobile and some had not. The key variable again was that of geographical mobility. I want therefore to widen the concept of social mobility to include geographical mobility, so that it is truly 'social' mobility and not just occupational-status mobility. Because I examined closely the social relationships of two groups living as neighbours I was able to identify the important factors but if I had followed the usual methodology for the study of social mobility this would not have been possible.

That the concept of social mobility should be enlarged to include some notion of geographical mobility so that theoretical categories are not only theoretical but are real groups, has recently had some independent empirical support. Elias and Scotson in their *The Established and The Outsiders* graphically show the importance of geographical mobility. Those they call 'the established' have neither been socially nor geographically mobile and correspond to those I call the locals (boxes number seven and eight in Table 8:1); 'the outsiders' are those that have been geographically mobile, and may or may not have been socially mobile as usually defined, and correspond to those I call the non-locals (boxes number one, two, five and six). Their analysis also shows that my model of mobility, Table 8:1, is relevant to the working class and not just to the middle class.

Methodologically, mobility studies must be closely involved with empirical field work. If Glass's data on mobility had been used in a community setting (as at one time it looked as if it would be with Bottomore's study of 'Squirebridge', published as Chapter XIII of the Glass volume), it is quite likely that geographical mobility would have been included sooner in the overall concept of 'social' mobility.

Margaret Stacey's concepts of traditional and non-traditional social systems in Banbury are closely involved with geographical mobility. The non-traditional members of the working class often had been geographically mobile, they were immigrants to the town whereas the traditional working class had not been geographically mobile, they were typically Banburians born and bred, The non-traditional middle class often had been both socially and geographically mobile, but they were predominantly newcomers to the town. By Blau's or Glass's methods many immigrant manual workers, those Mrs. Stacey calls non-traditional, would not have been socially mobile. Blau would have called them 'stationary lows'. Surely, however, they had been 'socially' mobile in the true sense of the term, even if they had not moved up the occupational-status hierarchy.

Finally I must conclude by returning to my point of departure, that of Watson's provocative introduction of the terms spiralist and burgess, and in particular to his introduction of the term spiralism for social mobility involving geographical mobility. This I feel is a major breakthrough in the study of mobility, but it must not be allowed to completely overshadow the previous studies. Watson has shown that a concept of social mobility that ignores geographical mobility as does that of Glass, Lipset and Bendix, and Blau will be inadequate. However to underemphasize the importance of intergenerational social (occupational) mobility, as there is a tendency to do in Watson's paper, is equally dangerous. My analysis of the effects of geographical mobility and social (occupational) mobility on

1. the extended family
2. the neighbourhood

shows that neither are adequate in themselves to understand and explain the social relationships of and between the 120 families studied. It was necessary to have a concept of 'social' mobility that included both these hitherto separate mobilities. The next task is to widen the application of this concept of a truly 'social' mobility to the study of other groups in society.

# References Cited

AARONOVITCH, s., *The Ruling Class*, Lawrence and Wishart, 1961.

ABERLE, D. F. and NAEGELE, K. O., 'Middle Class Fathers' Occupational Role and Attitudes towards Children', *Amer. J. of Orth. Psy.*, Vol. 22, 1952.

ARENSBURG, C. and KIMBALL, S., *Community and Culture*, Harcourt, Brace and World, 1965.

AXELROD, M., 'Urban Structure and Social Participation', *American Sociological Review*, 1956.

BABCHUK, N. and BATES, A., 'The Primary Relations of Middle-Class Couples: a study in male dominance', *American Sociological Review*, Vol. XXIII, 1963.

BANKS, J. A., 'Moving up in Society', *Twentieth Century*, May 1960.

BANTON, M., 'Social Distance, a new appreciation', *Sociological Review*, Vol. 8 (N.S.), 1960.

BANTON, M. (ed.), *The Social Anthropology of Complex Societies*, A.S.A. Monograph 4, Tavistock, 1966.

BARBER, B., *Social Stratification*, Harcourt, Brace, 1957.

BEALEY, F., BLONDEL, J. and MCCANN, W. P., *Constituency Politics: a study of Newcastle-under-Lyme*, Faber, 1965.

BERGER, B. M., *Working Class Suburb*, University of California Press, 1960.

BERGER, B. M., 'The Myth of Suburbia', *Journal of Social Issues*, Vol. 17, 1961.

BIRCH, A. M., *Small-Town Politics*, Oxford U.P., 1959.

BLAU, P. M., 'Social Mobility and Interpersonal Relations', *American Sociological Review*, Vol. XXI, pp. 290-5, 1956.

BOGARDUS, E. S., *Immigration and Race Attitudes*, D. C. Heath, 1928.

BOGARDUS, E. S., 'A Social Distance Scale', *Sociology and Social Research*, Vol. 17, pp. 265–71, 1933.

BOTT, E., *Family and Social Network*, Tavistock, 1957.

BRACEY, H., *Neighbours*, Routledge and Kegan Paul, 1964.

BRENNAN, T., COONEY, E. and POLLINS, H., *Social Change in South-West Wales*, Watts, 1954.

BROOM, L. and SMITH, J. H., 'Bridging Occupations', *British Journal of Sociology*, Vol. XIV, 1963.

BUTLER, D. E. and KING, A., *The British General Election: 1964*, Macmillan, 1965.

CAPLOW, T. and FORMAN, R., 'Neighbourhood Interaction in a Homogeneous Community', *American Sociological Review*, Vol. XV, 1950.

CARLSSON, G., *Social Mobility and Class Structure*, Lund, 1956.

CARLSSON, G. with GLASS, D. V. and SVALASTOGA, K., *Acta Sociologica*, Vol. 9, 1966.

CARTER, H., *The Towns of Wales*, University of Wales Press, 1965.

CHINOY, E., *Automobile Workers and the American Dream*, Doubleday, 1955.

CHRISTOPHER, S. C., 'A Research Note', *Int. J. Comparative Sociology*, Vol. 6, 1965.

COLE, G. D. H., 'The Conception of the Middle Classes', *British Journal of Sociology*, Vol. 1, 1950.

COLLISON, P. and MOGEY, J. N., 'Residence and Social Class in Oxford', *American Journal of Sociology*, Vol. 64, pp. 599–605, 1959.

COLLISON, P., *The Cuttleslowe Walls*, Faber, 1963.

CROZIER, D., 'Kinship and Occupational Succession', *Sociological Review*, Vol. 14 (N.S.), 1965.

CULLINGWORTH, J. B., *English Housing Trends*, Occasional Paper of Social Administration, No. 13, 1965.

DAHRENDORF, R., *Class and Class Conflict in Industrial Society*, Routledge and Kegan Paul, 1959.

DALTON, M., *Men who Manage*, Wiley, 1959.

DENNIS, N., 'The Popularity of the Neighbourhood Community Idea', *Sociological Review*, Vol. 6 (N.S.), 1958.

DOBRINER, W. M., *Class and Suburbia*, Prentice-Hall, 1963.

DOLLARD, J., *Class and Caste in a Southern Town*, Doubleday, 1937.

DONNISON, D. V., 'The Movement of Households in England',

*J. Royal Statistical Society* (series A), Vol. 124, pt. 1, pp. 60–80, 1961.

DURANT, R., *Watling: a survey of social life on a New Housing Estate*, King, 1939.

ELIAS, N. and SCOTSON, J. L., *The Established and The Outsiders*, Cass, 1965.

EPSTEIN, A. L., 'The Network and Urban Social Organisation', *Rhodes-Livingstone Journal*, No. 29, pp. 28–62, 1961.

FAVA, S. L., 'Suburbanism as a Way of Life', *American Sociological Review*, Vol. XXI, 1956.

FESTINGER, L., SCHACHTER, S. and BACK, K., *Social Pressures in Informal Groups*, Harper, 1950.

FIRTH, R., *Elements of Social Organisation*, Cohen and West, 1951.

FIRTH, R. (ed.), *Two Studies of Kinship in London*, L.S.E. Monograph on Social Anthropology, No. 15, 1956.

FIRTH, R., 'Introduction to Family and Kin Ties in Britain and their Sociological Importance', *British Journal of Sociology*, Vol. XII, 1961.

FIRTH, R., 'Family and Kinship in Industrial Society', pp. 65–87 of HALMOS (ed.), 1964.

FLETCHER, R., *Family and Marriage*, Penguin Special, 1962.

FLOUD, J., HALSEY, A. H. and MARTIN, F. M., *Social Class and Educational Opportunity*, Heinemann, 1957.

FORM, W. H., 'Status Stratification in a Planned Community', *American Sociological Review*, Vol. X, pp. 605–13, 1945.

FORM, W. H., 'Stratification in Low and Middle income Housing Areas', *Social Forces*, Vol. VII, pp. 109–31, 1951.

FRANKENBERG, R., 'Participant Observers', *New Society*, No. 23 (7.3.1963), 1963.

FRANKENBERG, R., *British Community Studies: problems of Synthesis*, pp. 123–54 of BANTON (1966) (ed.), Tavistock, 1966a.

FRANKENBERG, R., *British Communities: Social Life in Town and Country*, Pelican, 1966b.

GANS, H. J., 'Planning and Social Life; friendship and neighbor relations in Suburban Communities', *J. of American Institute of Planners*, Vol. 27, 1961.

GELLNER, E., *Thought and Change*, Weidenfeld and Nicholson, 1964.

GLASS, D. V., *et al.*, *Social Mobility in Britain*, Routledge and Kegan Paul, 1954.

GLUCKMAN, M., 'Analysis of a Social Situation in Modern Zululand', *Rhodes-Livingstone Paper No. 28*, 1940, 1942 and 1958.

GLUCKMAN, M., 'Ethnographic Data in British Social Anthropology', *Sociological Review*, Vol. 9 (N.S.), 1961.

GLUCKMAN, M., 'Gossip and Scandal', *Current Anthropology*, Vol. 4, 1963.

GLUCKMAN, M. and DEVONS, E. (eds.), *Closed Systems and Open Minds*, Oliver and Boyd, 1964.

GLUCKMAN, M. and EGGAN, F., *Introduction* to A.S.A. Monographs 1, 2, 3 and 4, BANTON (1966) (ed.), Tavistock, 1966.

GOFFMAN, E., *Asylums*, Doubleday, 1963.

GOLDSHMIDT, W., 'Social Class in America: a critical review', *American Anthropologist*, Vol. 57, 1950.

GREENFIELD, S. M., 'Industrialisation and the Family in Sociological Theory', *American Journal of Sociology*, Vol. 67, pp. 312–322, 1962.

GREER, S., 'Urbanism Reconsidered', *American Sociological Review*, Vol. XXI, 1956.

HALSEY, A. H., 'Reply to Turner', *American Sociological Review*, Vol. XXVI, 1961.

HALMOS, P. (ed.), 'The Development of Industrial Societies', *Sociological Review. Monograph No. 8*, 1964.

HAMILTON, R., 'The Income Difference between Skilled and White Collar Workers', *British Journal of Sociology*, Vol. 14, 1963.

HARRINGTON, M., 'Resettlement and Self Image', *Human Relations*, Vol. 18, pp. 115–37, 1965.

HARRIS, C. C., 'Locality Studies and Social Systems', unpublished paper presented to B.S.A. Conference Sept. 1965, 1965.

HERBERT, D. T., 'An approach to the study of the town as a central place', *Sociological Review*, Vol. 9 (N.S.), 1961.

HILTON, K. J., 'The Lower Swansea Valley Project', *Geography*, Vol. XLVIII, 1963.

HOGGART, R., *The Uses of Literacy*, Chatto and Windus, 1957.

HOLLINGSHEAD, A. B. and REDLICH, F. C., *Social Class and mental illness: a community study*, Chapman and Hall, 1958.

HOMANS, G., *Sentiments and Activities*, Routledge and Kegan Paul, 1962.

HUBERT, J., 'Kinship and Geographical Mobility in a Sample

from a London Middle-Class Area', *Int. J. Comparative Sociology*, Vol. 6, 1965.

JACKSON, E. F. and CROCKETT, H. J., 'Occupation Mobility in the United States', *American Sociological Review*, Vol. XXIX, 1964.

JACO, E. G. and BELKNAP, J., 'Is a new family form emerging in the urban fringe', *American Sociological Review*, Vol. XVIII, pp. 551–7, 1953.

KAHN, J. A., *The American Class Structure*, Holt, Reinhart and Winston, 1957.

KLEIN, J., *Samples from English Cultures*, 2 vols., Routledge and Kegan Paul, 1965.

LANCASTER, L., 'Some Conceptual Problems in the study of Family and Kin ties in the British Isles', *British Journal of Sociology*, Vol. 12, 1961.

LARSEN, O. N. and EDELSTEIN, A. S., 'Communication, Consensus and the Community Involvement of Urban Husbands and Wives', *Acta Sociologica*, Vol. 5, 1961.

LEWIS, O., *Life in a Mexican Village: Tepoztlan restudied*, University of Illinois Press, 1951.

LIPSET, S. M., 'Social Mobility and Urbanization', *Rural Sociology*, Vol. 20, 1954.

LIPSET, S. M. and BENDIX, R., *Social Mobility in Industrial Society*, Heinemann, 1959.

LIPSET, S. M., *Political Man*, Heinemann, 1959.

LITTLEJOHN, J., *Westrigg*, Routledge and Kegan Paul, 1963.

LITWAK, E., 'The use of Extended Family Groups in the Achievement of Social Goals', *Social Problems*, Vol. 7, 1960a.

LITWAK, E., 'Geographic Mobility and Extended Family Cohesion', *American Sociological Review*, Vol. XXV, 1960b.

LITWAK, E., 'Occupational Mobility and Extended Family Cohesion', *American Sociological Review*, Vol. XXV, 1960c.

LITWAK, E., 'Reference Group Theory, Bureaucratic Career and Neighborhood Primary Group Cohesion', *Sociometry*, Vol. 23, 1960d.

LITWAK, E. and FELLIN, P., 'Neighborhood Cohesion under Conditions of Mobility', *American Sociological Review*, Vol. XXVIII, 1963.

LLOYD, M. G. and THOMASON, G. F., *Welsh Society in Transition*, The Council of Social Service for Wales and Monmouthshire, 1963.

LOCKWOOD, D., *The Black Coated Worker*, Allen and Unwin.

LOCKWOOD, D., 'Sources of Variation in Working Class Images of Society', *Sociological Review*, Vol. 14, 1966.

LOUDON, J. B., 'Kinship and Crises in South Wales', *British Journal of Sociology*, Vol. 12, 1961.

LOUDON, J. B., *Religious Order and Mental Disorder*, pp. 69–96 of A.S.A. 4, BANTON (1966) (ed.), Tavistock, 1966.

LYDALL, R. F. and TIPPING, D. G., 'The Distribution of Personal Wealth in Britain', *Oxford University Institute of Statistics Bulletin*, Vol. 23, 1961.

MACRAE, D. G., *Ideology and Society*, Heinemann, 1961.

MACRAE, N., 'The Faults in the Dynamos: a probe into "the men at the top" ', *Encounter*, July 1965.

MANN, P., 'The Concept of Neighborliness', *American Journal of Sociology*, Vol. 60, 1954.

MANN, P., *An Approach to Urban Sociology*, Routledge and Kegan Paul, 1965.

MANNERS, G., 'Service Industries and Regional Economic Growth', *Town Planning Review*, Vol. 33, 1963.

MANNERS, G. (ed.), *South Wales in the Sixties*, Pergamon, 1964.

MANNHEIM, K., *Man and Society in an age of Reconstruction*, translated by SHILS, E. A., Routledge and Kegan Paul, 1940.

MARSH, R. M., *The Mandarins: the circulation of elites in China*, Free Press of Glencoe, 1961.

MARX, K., *The Eighteenth Brumaire of Louis-Napoleon*, Translated by DE LEON, D., Foreign Publishing House, 1898.

MAYER, A., *The Significance of Quasi-Groups in the Study of Complex Societies*, A.S.A. 4, pp. 97–122 of BANTON (1966) (ed.), 1966.

MERTON, R. K., *The Social Psychology of Housing*, University of Pittsburg Press, 1943.

MERTON, R. K., *Social Theory and Social Structure*, Free Press of Glencoe, 1957.

MERTON, R. K. and NESBIT, R. A. (eds.), *Contemporary Social Problems*, Harcourt, Brace, 1963.

MILLER, S. M., 'Comparative Social Mobility', *Current Sociology*, Vol. 9, 1960.

MILLS, C. WRIGHT, Review of WARNER (1941), *American Sociological Review*, Vol. VII, 1942.

MILLS, C. WRIGHT, *The Sociological Imagination*, Oxford U.P., 1959.

MITCHELL, J. CLYDE, 'The Kalela Dance', *Rhodes-Livingstone Paper* No. 27, 1956.

MITCHELL, J. CLYDE, *Introduction* to van Velson (1964), Manchester U.P., 1964.

MITCHELL, J. CLYDE, *Theoretical Orientations in African Urban Studies*, pp. 37–68 of A.S.A. 4, BANTON (1966) (ed.), Tavistock, 1966.

MORGAN, K. V., *Swansea West*, pp. 265–77 of BUTLER and KING (1965), Macmillan, 1965.

MORRIS, R. N. and MOGEY, J., *The Sociology of Housing*, Routledge and Kegan Paul, 1965.

MORRIS, R. T. and MURPHY, R. J., 'The Situs Dimension in the Occupational Structure', *American Sociological Review*, Vol. XXIV, pp. 231–9, 1959.

MOWRER, E. R., 'Sequential and Class Variables of the Family in Suburban Areas', *Social Forces*, Vol. 40, pp. 107–12, 1961.

MUMFORD, L., *The Culture of Cities*, Secker and Warburg, 1946.

MUMFORD, L., *The City in History*, Secker and Warburg, 1963.

MUSGROVE, F., *The Migratory Elite*, Heinemann, 1963.

OSTERREICH, H., 'Geographic Mobility and Kinship: a Canadian Example', *Int. J. Comparative Sociology*, Vol. 6, 1965.

PAHL, R., *Urbs in Rure*, L.S.E. Geography Monographs No. 2, 1964.

PAHL, R., 'Class and Community in English Commuter Villages', *Socialogis Ruralis*, Vol. 2, 1965.

PARSONS, T., *The Social System*, Free Press of Glencoe, 1951.

PLOWMAN, G., MINCHINTON, W. and STACEY, M., 'Local Status in England and Wales', *Sociological Review*, Vol. 10 (N.S.), 1962.

PONS, V., *Two Small Groups in Avenue 21*, in SOUTHALL (1961) (ed.), Oxford U.P., 1961.

RADCLIFFE-BROWN, A. R., *Structure and Function in Primitive Society*, Cohen and West, 1952.

REES, G., 'Have the Welsh a Future?', *Encounter*, March 1964.

REGISTRAR-GENERAL, *Migration*: National Summary Tables, Part I and II, 1965.

RICHMOND, A., 'Back From Canada', *New Society*, No. 123 (4.2. 1965), 1965.

ROSSER, C. and HARRIS, C. C., 'Relationships through Marriage in a Welsh Urban Area', *Sociological Review*, Vol. 9 (N.S.), 1961.

ROSSER, C. and HARRIS, C. C., *The Family and Social Change*, Routledge and Kegan Paul, 1965.

ROSSI, P. H., *Why Families Move*, Free Press of Glencoe, 1955.

RUNCIMAN, W. G., *Relative Deprivation and Social Justice*, Routledge and Kegan Paul, 1966.

SAMPSON, A., *Anatomy of Britain Today*, Hodder and Stoughton, 1964.

SCHEIDER, L. and LYSGAARD, S., 'The Deferred Gratification Pattern', *American Sociological Review*, Vol. XVIII, 1953.

SCHNEIDER, D. M., and HOMANS, G. C., 'Kinship Terminology and the American Kinship System', *American Anthropologist*, Vol. 59, 1955.

SCHUMPETER, J., *Imperialism and Social Classes*, Blackwell, 1951.

SEELEY, J. R., SIM, R. A. and LOOSLEY, E. W., *Crestwood Heights*, Wiley, 1963.

SHAW, L. A., 'Impressions of Family Life in a London Suburb', *Sociological Review*, Vol. 2 (N.S.), 1954.

SOROKIN, P. R., *Social Mobility*, Free Press of Glencoe, 1927.

SOUTHALL, A. (ed.), *Social Change in Modern Africa*, Oxford U.P., 1961.

SPENCE, S., *Lower Swansea Valley Project Report*, A Study of Land Use in a Regional Context, 1964.

SPROTT, W. J. H., *Human Groups*, Pelican, 1958.

STACEY, B. G., 'Some Psychological Aspects of Inter-generational Occupational Mobility', *Brit. J. Soc. Clin. Psychol.*, 4, 1965.

STACEY, B. G., 'Some Psychological Aspects of Inter-generational Mobility', *Human Relations*, Vol. 20, No. 1, 1967.

STACEY, M., *Tradition and Change: a study of Banbury*, Oxford U.P., 1961.

STACEY, M., 'Lower Swansea Valley Project Report', *Housing Report*, 1965a.

STACEY, M., 'Local Studies and Social Systems', unpublished paper presented to B.S.A. Conference, Sept. 1965, 1965b.

STEIN, M., *The Eclipse of Community: some glances at the education of a sociologist*, pp. 207–32 of VIDICH, BENSMAN and STEIN (1964), Wiley, 1964.

STOUFFER, S., 'Interviewing Opportunities: a theory relating mobility and distance', *American Sociological Review*, Vol. V, 1940.

STRAUSS, M. H., 'Deferred Gratification, Social Class and Achievement Syndrome', *American Sociological Review*, Vol. XXVII, 1962.

SUSSER, M. and WATSON, A., *Sociology in Medicine*, Oxford U.P., 1962.

SUSSMAN, M. B., 'The Help Pattern of the Middle Class Family', *American Sociological Review*, Vol. XVIII, 1953.

SUSSMAN, M. B. and WHITE, R. C., *Hough, Cleveland, Ohio: a study of social life and change*, Western Reserve U.P., 1959.

SUSSMAN, M. B. and BURCHINAL, L., 'Kin Family Network: Unheralded Structure in Current Conceptualization of Family Functioning', *Marriage and Family Living*, Vol. 24, 1962.

SYKES, A. J. M., 'Some differences in the Attitude of Clerical and Manual Workers', *Sociological Review*, Vol. 13 (N.S.), 1965.

TAUSKY, C. and DUBIN, R., 'Career Anchorage: Managerial Mobility Motivations,' *American Sociological Review*, Vol. XXX, 1965.

THERNSTROM, S., *Poverty and Progress: social mobility in a nineteenth century city*, Harvard U.P., 1964.

TOWNSEND, P., *The Family Life of Old People*, Pelican, 1963.

TOWNSEND, P., Discussant to FIRTH (1964) in HALMOS (1964) (ed.), 1964.

TUCKER, J., *Honourable Estates*, Gollancz, 1966.

TURNER, V. W., *Schism and Continuity in an African Society*, Manchester U.P., 1957.

VELSEN, J. VAN, *The Politics of Kinship*, Manchester U.P., 1964.

VIDICH, A. J., 'Participant Observation and the Collection and Interpretation of Data', *American Journal of Sociology*, Vol. 60, 1954.

VIDICH, A. J., BENSMAN, J. and STEIN, M., *Reflections upon Community Studies*, Wiley, 1964.

WARNER, J. LLOYD, *The Social Life of a Modern Community*, Yankee City Series, Vol. I, Yale U.P., 1941.

WARNER, J. LLOYD, et al., *Democracy in Jonesville*, Harper Torchbooks, 1949.

WARNER, J. LLOYD and ABEGGLEN, J. C., *Occupation Mobility in American Business and Industry, 1928–1952*, 1955.

WATSON, W., 'The Managerial Spiralist', *Twentieth Century*, May 1960.

WATSON, W., *Social Mobility and Social Class in Industrial Communities*, in GLUCKMAN and DEVONS, Oliver and Boyd, 1964.

WEBER, M., *The Theory of Social and Economic Organisation*, translated by HENDERSON, A. M. and PARSONS, T., Free Press of Glencoe, 1947.

WEISS, R. S. and REISMAN, D., *Social Problems and Disorganisation in the world of Work*, in MERTON and NESBIT (1963) (eds.), Harcourt, Brace, 1963.

WEST, W., *Plainville: U.S.A.*, Columbia U.P., 1945.

WHYTE, W. H., *The Organisation Man*, Jonathan Cape, 1956.

WILLIAMS, R., Conversation (with R. HOGGART), *New Left Review*, No. I, 1960.

WILLIAMS, W. M., *The Sociology of an English Village: Gosforth*, Routledge and Kegan Paul, 1956.

WILLIAMS, W. M., *A West Country Village*, Routledge and Kegan Paul, 1963.

WILLIAMS, W. M. and HERBERT, D. F., 'Social Geography of Newcastle-under-Lyme', *North Staffordshire Field Journal*, 1963.

WILLMOTT, P., 'Kinship and Social Legislation', *British Journal of Sociology*, Vol. 9, 1958.

WILLMOTT, P. and YOUNG, M., *Family and Class in a London Suburb*, Routledge and Kegan Paul, 1960.

YOUNG, M. and WILLMOTT, P., *Family and Kin in East London*, Routledge and Kegan Paul, 1957.

ZELDICH, M., 'Some Methodological Problems of Field Studies', *American Journal of Sociology*, Vol. 67, 1962.

# The *Aide Mémoire*

The *aide mémoire* was changed slightly several times during the fieldwork but there are certain 'core' parts that were retained throughout. These included the questions designed to elicit the basic demographic data, the household's residential and education history, and certain aspects of the husband's career, also the details of kin contact and distribution. These data are presented for all 120 families in the book. Much of the material that I gathered I have not used, as will become apparent from the following.

## Introduction

1. Are you Welsh? If YES: do you speak Welsh?
   to whom and when?
   Did/do either of your parents speak Welsh?
   to whom and when?
   Do any of your children speak Welsh?
   to whom and when?
2. Do you like living in Wales? in Swansea? on this estate?

## Residential Mobility

3. Why did you come to this particular estate?
4. How long have you lived here?
5. Where did you live before you came here?
6. How many times have you moved since you started work? (Why each time?)
7. Where were you brought up?
8. Do you think that you will move again? Why? When? Where to?
9. Do you rent/own this house? How many previous houses have you owned?

## The Estate

10. What kind of people live on this estate? How would you describe them?

11. Is there any social life on the estate?
12. How did you get to know people?
13. Whose houses have you been into? What for and when?
14. Who do you (the housewife) see during a normal day?
15. Do people on this estate help each other? In what way?
16. Who are you friendly with on the estate?

## Demography

17. Who lives in this house? ages?
18. How long have you been married?

## Occupational and Educational History

19. What is your occupation? 'tell me about it' (how often moved firm and place of work).
20. How many employees has your firm?
21. How many branches has your firm?
22. Wife's job.
23. What type of school did you attend?
24. When did you leave? 'O' or 'A' levels.
25. University? Other post-school education.

## Kin

Will you tell me about your family?
26. Father's occupation when you started work? at 60?
27. Where do your parents live, when did you last see them?
28. Where do your brothers live, when did you last see them?
29. Where do your sisters live, when did you last see them?
30. Where do your children (if not living with them) live, etc.?
31. Where do your uncles live, when did you last see them?
32. Where do your aunts live, when did you last see them?
33. What are the occupation of those who are working (or their husbands)?
34. When did you last see a lot of your relatives?
35. Do your family help each other (prompt: about housing? with money for children).
36. Is there a relative of yours working in the same firm as you?

## Friend

37. Where does your 'best friend' live?
38. When did you last see him/her?
39. How did you meet him/her?
40. What is his/her job? (or husband's job?)
41. Where do they live?

## Crises

42. If the wife was ill in bed what would happen? Would anyone come to help? Who? (Ask about actual situations wherever possible.)
43. What happened to your family when the last child was born?

## Leisure

44. Do you belong to any clubs/societies/associations?
45. Do you belong to a church or chapel? When did you last attend?
46. What did you do over Christmas, New Year?
47. Do you use the public library?
48. What do you do for your holidays?

## General

49. What papers/magazines do you take?
50. Have you got a car/telephone/boat?
51. What do you feel about the Welsh Nationalist?
52. Are you in favour of the introduction of comprehensive Schools in Swansea?
53. Who did you vote for at the last General Election?
54. What is your income?
55. What social class would you say you belonged to? (if you had to say middle or working class which would you say?)
56. What sort of people do you mean by middle or working class?
57. Do you think differences in social class are still significant today?— more important say than the differences between English and Welsh in Swansea?

## Comments

Only very rarely were the questions asked in the order they are printed above. As far as possible I tried to talk round each topic and usually it would take several interviews to cover all the questions.

# Welsh Speaking

I was interested in Welsh speaking not in itself but as an index of a cultural orientation. In fact it did not appear to be at all significant in the structure of social relations, either on or off the estate. The local/non-local division cut across the Welsh speaking/non-Welsh speaking division.

In my definitions I followed Rosser and Harris (1965) who wrote (p. 120): 'if both the subject and his parents could not speak any Welsh at all, we placed him in our "non-Welsh" category: the remainder (that is those who could themselves speak Welsh either fluently or partly and who had one or both parents speaking some Welsh) formed our "Welsh" category.'

Rosser and Harris obtained the following two-way table:

|  |  | PARENTS WELSH SPEAKING | |
|---|---|---|---|
|  |  | SOME | NONE |
| SUBJECTS WELSH | SOME | 457 | 100 |
| SPEAKING | NONE | 339 | 1061 |

∴ non-Welsh = 54% of their sample.
  Welsh    = 46% of their sample.

The 120 families that I studied could be broken down in the following way:

|  |  | PARENTS WELSH SPEAKING | |
|---|---|---|---|
|  |  | SOME | NONE |
| SUBJECTS WELSH | SOME | 26 | 2 |
| SPEAKING | NONE | 19 | 193 |

∴ the non-Welsh = 80% of my families.
  Welsh       = 20% of my families.

Using this definition and those previously developed for social and geographical mobility, the following table can be obtained (using households

184

as units, the characteristics of the household being determined by the husband):

| | NON-LOCALS | | LOCALS | |
| | *Socially immobile and geographically mobile* | *Socially and geographically mobile* | *Socially and geographically immobile* | *Totals* |
|---|---|---|---|---|
| NON-WELSH | 54 | 27 | 15 | 96 |
| WELSH | 15 | 4 | 5 | 24 |
| Totals | 69 | 31 | 20 | 120 |

From this it can be seen that by no means all the locals were Welsh as defined, and also that not all the non-locals were non-Welsh. Nevertheless, on both estates the locals were known as 'the Welsh'.

# Index

# Index